THE ANATOMY OF UHURU

The Anatomy of Uhuru

DYNAMICS AND PROBLEMS OF AFRICAN
INDEPENDENCE IN AN AGE OF CONFLICT

by

N. S. CAREY JONES

FREDERICK A. PRAEGER, *Publishers*
New York · Washington

BOOKS THAT MATTER

Published in the United States of America in 1967
by Frederick A. Praeger, Inc., Publishers
111 Fourth Avenue, New York, N.Y 10003

First published in Great Britain in 1966
by Manchester University Press,
316–324 Oxford Road, Manchester 13, England

Library of Congress Catalog Card Number: 67–12789

Printed in Great Britain

Contents

Preface

WHAT follows was written in November 1964, nearly a year after Kenya's independence. Most of the footnotes have been added since. There has been little need in the ensuing months to bring it up to date, since the more significant changes that have taken place are forecast in it: the one-party state; the failure of proposals for E.A. federation; and the control of the trade unions. The E.A. common market does not as yet seem to have disintegrated altogether, but Kenya is setting up its own central bank and seems to be facing foreign exchange problems.

While I imagine that they would accept very few of my conclusions, I owe an immense debt to Max and Mary Gluckman who, many years ago in Livingstone, stimulated me to think about what was going on around me. I am also grateful to them for reading and commenting on the original manuscript.

N.S.C.J.

Leeds, 1966

CHAPTER ONE

Introduction

Two figures walk at midnight to the centre of a brightly lit stadium. An old flag is lowered and a new one is raised as an old and a new national anthem are played. A vast crowd cheers. There is an outburst of fireworks. Dancing is renewed—significantly, perhaps, tribal dancing. Some are sad at the passing of an empire. Most rejoice as a new world of a million hopes is opened. Within a few days the decorations will have gone, the stadium will have been pulled down. People will have returned to their ordinary business.

What has really happened at this ceremony? Is it no more than a symbol that a country has changed course so far that the new direction needs formal recognition, the replacement of old symbols by new? Has, perhaps, nothing really changed and is the country moving under the same forces as gave it direction before? Will the same forces that brought it to this point of independence continue to govern its course? Will some of them fall away and others increase? Or have new forces been released and are they for good or evil? Has some new Pandora's box been opened with a million evils and only one hope or are there new opportunities to channel a great release of energy to good ends? Why did it happen at all? Where are its springs—in Africa, in Britain, in America, in the United Nations, in Moscow or even Peking? Were the people, in fact, powerless not to be independent? Did events move from the arrival of the first Europeans in Kenya to *Uhuru* with the inevitability of a Greek tragedy? Did, perhaps, those who were most against it do most to promote it? Is it really independence or a new

I

dependence? Will an African government be, in fact, as helpless as a colonial government, which was always the resultant of the forces acting upon it, or even more so? How far are those forces different now?

This essay is an attempt to disentangle the threads that went to bring about this thing called *uhuru*; to see what their strength is and to estimate how far they are likely to influence it in the future. Some of the threads are peculiar to Kenya so that what is said will not be valid for other African countries. The main threads are undoubtedly common to most African countries. Some are common to former British colonies but not to French or Portuguese colonies.

Almost any simile that is adopted to describe *uhuru* can be misleading. Is it a tangled knot of which the threads must be unravelled in order to understand how it is made up? This is too static and knots can be unravelled. A ball of many-coloured plasticine is better. It indicates how mixed and blended are the colours that make up the predominant hues and it emphasizes that they cannot be separated. Again, however, it is too static. A country is never still. It receives forces, impulses, pressures—call them what you will—which determine at any moment its direction. These forces give it a momentum so that it is not easily deflected suddenly from its previous course. Sudden deflections occur where an accumulation of forces overcome the momentum or where other forces are withdrawn and a new direction and momentum become evident. *Uhuru* marks such a point in time. It is however, only a deflection. Old forces are still present. What seem new forces were often there before. New ones will arise which will affect it in the future. Its new momentum may be not a straight line but a curve. All this, perhaps, is no more than saying that Kenya is a part of the world and influenced by it, although the influence is tempered by local forces.

This is not to deny the importance of the individual. He,

too, however, is influenced by these same forces and pressures. He derives his ideas from them. The individual in action is not a philosopher. He can affect the forces at work but mainly he can only express them. Particularly he can affect the timing of their results. Sometimes he can harness and express latent forces that are not apparent to others, but this is rare. He can identify himself with a particular force and give it greater strength and influence in affairs, often most successfully if his identification is not common knowledge. He may simply hitch his own personal wagon to a particular force and ride to personal success or go down to defeat with it. He may try to ride several forces in harness and his success will depend on his choosing a group that are not moving in different directions. The individual of personal convictions while not identifying himself with any force must be ready to use them, jumping from this to that to further his objects. This makes him very hard to distinguish from the man who is simply pursuing his own personal interests with skill. It is possible for an individual to work out, and work for, the national interest as something not identifiable with one or more of the forces playing on the nation. As he must use these it is not easy to be sure that he is not simply a self-seeker. The individual can only work through existing forces.

There is one exception to this; the use of physical force by the individual, assuming he has control of some. He can use physical force either to bring about changes or to resist them. Generally it will be the latter, since the control of physical force will tend to be in the hands of those who wish to resist internal change, but also, of course, in the hands of those who wish to cause change in other peoples. In his own country the national leader will express the forces making for change or resist change by the use of physical force. In other countries he may express change by the use of physical force; invasion, liberation armies, underground movements of intimidation or sabotage. Within a country sector leaders can also use physical force in support of change. All, except those with strong religious convictions (or pseudo-religious convictions) or fools, respond to physical force. While I may go to the stake for my God, if an armed robber attacks me, I hold up my hands and surrender my purse.

Physical force, then, can either advance or retard change. If it advances change it will set off new non-physical forces which will lead to further unpredictable, and often unintended changes. If it retards change it may even succeed in doing so for such a length of time that the change it was resisting loses some of its strength, or disappears, as yet new forces play on the country and move it in some new direction. It is essential to peace and order if not to progress. This is not immediately understood by revolutionary governments, which attain position (but not power) in the name of liberty, until they are superseded by those who understand the need for force. As the taxi-drivers of Nairobi said: 'After independence we shall drive where we like on the road, and not have to keep to the left.'

Physical force is a factor of importance which can affect any study of the other forces acting on a country and it will have to be considered in itself; how far it can be created and brought under the control of any individual or group.

History may be simple story-telling—what happened here or there at this or that point in time—and none the less interesting for that. It can be an instrument of moral, religious or national propaganda, designed to further a point of view, provide an example or extract a particular significance. Modern research points to much of the Bible being history extracted for its theological significance. The Bible is not history, or literature, as some publishers would have us believe, but theology illustrated in action. History again is the means of transmitting from one generation to the next the traditions and attitudes of the nation. It has an advantage over ballads, sagas and epics in that it can be re-written and adapted as the nation's ideas change. This does not mean that historians determine a nation's attitudes. They re-interpret and re-write history in the light of those attitudes. Modern historical work is the re-interpretation of records (and the seeking of new ones) in ways suggested by contemporary *mores*.

This is not to deny value to history, although where it has value it shades into sociology, psychology and economics. For the historian proper it is a study of cause and effect, an attempt to understand what trends, forces, pressures, etc., led to what results; why they did so; where they came from; how were they handled by men. The contemporary historian must have been sufficiently close to events to be able to recognize the meaningful signs which reveal the forces at play in the country—the symptoms. If he is too far removed he will miss these and see only results. If he is too involved personally he will see as significant what he is looking for, even if he is not, as an actor, concerned to justify his actions.

This is not the place to argue a philosophy of history but only to set out briefly the writer's own, so that the approach he is taking is known and understood. Contemporary history is often a matter of reading between the lines, of catching the significant aside in the formal statement. Most men betray their attitudes, their feelings, what moves them, not in their public or formal statements, even to a friend, but in the unconscious aside which is not relevant to the subject but is highly relevant to some other subject. Or a formal answer to one question may be logically inconsistent with the formal answer to another. This implies that both answers are rationalizations in particular circumstances of some deeper attitude or emotion which may be concealed even from the speaker himself. The contemporary historian is looking for these indications of real forces underneath; he is sensing trends rather than seeing them.

This is an apologia for an essay that will be given to generalization rather than fact, to historical interpretation rather than to history-writing. There will be significant examples given but not the material for a history of Kenya. It may be hoped that it will contribute to the understanding of events so that when the history comes to be written it will be sounder.

The weakness of generalization has been summed up in the dictum: all generalizations are false, including this one. It ignores detail. Anyone can think of any number of particular examples that do not fit the generalization. This does not mean that the generalization is meaningless. It only purports to extract a dominant theme from a mass of facts and to illustrate the theme from significant examples. Every onlooker interprets a scene differently and subjectively, as every reader of a book reads it selectively and sees a different significance in it. (What else would keep our professors of Eng. Lit. going and provide their students with doctoral theses?) The very classificatory tool that the analyst uses may give false results because the initial classifications used may be drawn up in such a way as to distort rather than clarify. There is probably no way out of this. One has to accept that, in the infinite complexity of human affairs, nothing can be proved. One can only hope that a strong presumption of fairness and soundness may be caused in the reader's mind. Fortunately, both are qualities that a large number of human minds can recognize, even though this capacity is weakened in some by self-interest, an emotional pre-disposition, or indoctrination with other things. At the best, perhaps, this essay can be no more than a contribution to thought on *uhuru*; better in some ways than that of the journalists who are not close enough to sense things or to know where to look for significance; better than the memoirs of the principals, who are too involved in the events they relate, both factually and emotionally, even if the memoirs are not self-justifications.

This is a study of *uhuru* in Kenya. My own limitations of knowledge and experience prevent it being more, although I shall draw on experience elsewhere when it is relevant. It will have some meaning for other countries, but the less as they are subject to more different forces and as their own circumstances differ. Many of the forces that play on Kenya also play on other countries, but countries with different internal forces and a different raw material base. The pattern of events in Kenya has some overall resemblance to the pattern of other countries, but could be misleading if too strictly applied to them.

We all know that it is wrong to make statements of the kind: he is a Russian, Jewish, English, African, etc., swindler, thief, liar, scoundrel, etc., because of the transference that is made (and often intended to be made) from the bad word to the nation, and that there are only swindlers, thieves, liars, scoundrels, etc., who may belong to any nation. I had hoped to avoid all general national or racial terms, but this is impossible without immense circumlocution. I shall, therefore, refer to Europeans, Asians, Africans and other groups and to subdivisions of these, and make generalizations about them, in the full knowledge that a great many in each group are outside the generalization. I am largely considering the attitudes of people, and groups are usually individuals expressing some (but not all) attitudes in common. Similarly I am compelled to use the expressions 'imperialist', 'colonialist', 'neo-colonialist', 'extremist'. These are not used in any positive way as the basis of a statement, but only to describe the noises made by those groups that use them for abuse.

Most people tell the truth about what they see, even when they are interested parties, but they only see a part, however brightly. Here one needs yet another simile—the many-faceted stone. The 'die-hard' settler and the African 'ex-tremist' each see one or more of the facets, often with brilliant clarity. The 'moderates' see others. All of them are correct in describing what they see, but it is only a part. The very clarity with which they see their parts makes it harder for them to see the whole. It would be foolish of me to claim to do so. The reader must judge whether the whole object is being described. It is an object which is changing shape all the time, and a facet too small to see now may become an important one in the future. Each major facet that I shall describe has an irregular surface with many minor facets.

But let us leave this new simile before it betrays us and return to our more abstract, but more dynamic, resultant of forces.

The main forces that I shall describe, apart from the basic social and economic geography (the raw material on which the forces play and which itself gives rise to forces) are the immigrant races (settler, official and commercial); the African (tribal and emergent); and the World (Britain, the U.S.A., the United Nations and the Communist East).

CHAPTER TWO

Raw Material Background

KENYA is often described in fifths or four-fifths. Four-fifths of the country is desert or semi-desert of no agricultural value. The remainder contains some of the richest agricultural land in Africa. It lies in the south-west corner on the slopes of Mount Kenya and the eastern slopes of the Aberdare Mountains (the home of the Kikuyu tribe) and on the slopes descending to the shores of Lake Victoria (the home of the Abaluhya and Luo tribes). These form the Highlands of Kenya, together with the land in between them. The only other parts with agricultural significance are the Coastal Strip (formerly part of the Sultanate of Zanzibar) and the small area at the top of the Teita Hills, 100 miles from the Coast.

THE COAST[1]

The Coastal Strip is narrow and has been settled by various immigrants for a long time, from the Arabs of the twelfth to thirteenth centuries. Records show that some Portuguese tried farming there four hundred years ago, but did not stay. The land is now owned by a variety of Arabs, Asians and Europeans. The government has for many years been adjudicating land title claims there, but the task is not yet completed. The adjudication has always been an early victim of economy campaigns in the capital, where other problems have seemed more urgent. No African tribes have held land there although individual Africans have come into

[1] The Coast covers more than the strip formerly under the suzerainty of the Sultan of Zanzibar.

possession of land through government settlement schemes, which have been growing slowly over many years. There are large areas of Crown Lands. (The latter are now, properly, Regional lands, but the use of the old term Crown Lands explains their nature more readily—lands neither alienated to individuals nor in customary tribal ownership.)

The Strip grows a variety of tree crops. The main products are cotton, sisal, sugar, cashewnuts and coconuts. Except for cashewnuts these are largely plantation crops. The climate is against sustained effort and efficiency and a large part of the Coast is relatively undeveloped, while the production of cashewnuts (and coconuts) varies with the price. Clearly the 'real' production does not do this, since trees do not know the price. Below a certain price it is not thought worth collecting the nuts and bringing them to market. This illustrates an important point. Nearly all African economic agriculture (production for the market) is combined with subsistence agriculture so that, with the family food supplies arranged, a considerable incentive in price is necessary if the extra effort is to be made to overcome the inertia caused (at the Coast) by the climate and (elsewhere) by the customary way of life.[1]

These factors are often overlooked, particularly by foreign economists. They explain why so much of African agriculture progresses so slowly. Life is easy at customary standards of living. Housing and fuel (for cooking only) are cheap. Clothing is decorative rather than necessary, nor does custom demand much of it. The farmer concentrates on producing food. Life is easy but work is hard. Needs are few and competition in the use of consumer-goods non-existent. Money for taxes and extras, clothes, pots, etc., can be obtained by going out to work at a time when the need to work in one's own field is small. Wealth is measured in possessions

[1] A similar situation governed coconut production in British Honduras. See my *The Pattern of a Dependent Economy* (C.U.P., 1953), p. 61.

that are only partly economic; having economic potential rather than being actually economic; land, cattle, trees. The change to a market economy requires a big incentive. Although in theory a very small marginal increase in production could produce a considerable increase in wealth and deployable cash, this is not achieved because economics are not thought of in these alien terms. We shall see, later, how these attitudes were broken through elsewhere in the country. No breakthrough has yet been achieved at the Coast.

Something of this attitude is reflected by the immigrant community at the Coast, even though its members have come from money-making environments. It would probably be true to say of all the immigrants to Kenya, outside the towns, that they are not competitive among themselves. They belong to an élite and are sufficiently superior to the mass not to feel the need to compete with each other in the display of wealth. They want to make money, because they are conditioned to do so, but they, too, balance effort and result. At the Coast the effort seems disproportionately great and the standard of living of the immigrants is relatively lower than elsewhere. What they do get from Kenya is a certain real freedom and independence, especially from custom. This is common to all colonies. The real lure is away from the restrictive customs and attitudes of the immigrant's own society rather than the prospect of wealth. All colonies have been remarkable for their number of eccentrics.

At the Coast this combination of circumstances has led to rather haphazard development. Some have pushed ahead with developing their estates; some have done the minimum development that will give them a reasonable income; some have done little or nothing at all. This explains why it was possible to start describing African attitudes to the market economy immediately after having stated that Africans do not own land at the Coast. There are large numbers of squatters on the under-developed lands, including the Crown Lands. There are few parts of the Coast that are not in some sort of more or less beneficial occupation. In many cases squatters have been on the same land for forty years or more and have planted their own trees. From time to time landowners have tried to enlist government support in evicting the squatters, more particularly as the adjudication of titles made its slow progress and the owners' rights became established. The government, at one point, established a fund for compensating those squatters who had planted tree crops on other persons' land, as an aid to eviction. Generally, however, the Coast continued to muddle along quietly, to the despair of those who wished to develop it and knew how to do so. The illegal squatter (to distinguish him from the Resident Labourer, also called a 'squatter') is an important element in the Kenya scene. Lack of development by owners gives him his opportunity. In turn he prevents further development. He is a subsistence agriculturalist seeking principally to feed himself and his family. At the Coast he has been so long established on alienated land ('alienated' land is land in individual ownership) that he is also, to some extent, a contributor to the market economy, but a half-hearted one. Without title to the land he occupies he cannot be brought fully into the market economy. He cannot borrow money or develop. To evict him, if there is no alternative employment, causes hardship. To leave him prevents development at the Coast and the creation of alternative employment.

Some development was slowly taking place and this was having its effects, so that the Coast illustrates, with differences, what has been happening elsewhere in Kenya. Money was going into the area, from sisal, coconuts, sugar and cashewnuts, and the people were beginning to have new wants. Although competitive consumption was at a low level it was beginning and would grow, but with the structural obstacles that were noted above. Production for the market was still something incidental to the basic way of life.

The cashewnut industry is an example of the organizational problems of development. Cashewnuts are exported raw to India for processing for the American market. The nut-shelling operation is highly labour-intensive and requires skill. Supplies of nuts within India have been insufficient to meet the demand and India purchases nuts up and down the East African coastline. Limited attempts have been made at processing in Kenya, but the local people have not achieved the skill and efficiency to be competitive with India and to sell direct to America. As a result, local processors have been unable to pay the same price for nuts as these obtain in the Indian market. Given a period of time they could gain the skills; but the processors need an assured supply during that period or the venture becomes too risky. To compete successfully with India would provide local employment on a large scale. To deal with this the government recently attempted to control the local market and ensure to the processors an adequate supply at a price that would make them competitive. This case demonstrates the need for organized regulation of the market, particularly to overcome the lack of skill and knowledge. It shows the heave that is required to set up an industry in a country which is behindhand. It also shows the competitiveness of all tropical primary producers, since the successful establishment of the industry in Kenya would impoverish India by the same amount. The obstacles to catching up on skills and knowledge condemn a backward country to remaining behind unless it has, on the one hand, entrepreneurs prepared to venture into what are basically small-scale enterprises but of great local importance, and, on the other hand, an efficient administrative machine to regulate the economy to the extent needed to remove the obstacle. Completely free enterprise cannot solve this problem, which requires time. The significance of this in relation to *uhuru* in Kenya is the effect, which we shall see later, of *uhuru* on the availability of small entrepreneurs, or big entrepreneurs prepared to undertake small enterprises, and on the government administrative machinery. Matters of this kind, small in themselves, require an organization that can apply very detailed solutions and apply them effectively so that they do not turn to excessive gain for some at the expense of others.

Why is it necessary to provide employment if life is easy and needs are few? The answer to this is twofold. Firstly, medical attention is cheap or free. The population grows in the absence of tribal wars and slavery and with a reduction in disease. The early penetration of the market economy, however small, circulates money and provides some protection against natural calamities. Life will not always be easy. Governments must try to develop resources and production so that new activities will be created to engage the growing population. Secondly, the circulation of money does slowly have its effects on consumer habits. The demand for consumer goods begins to appear. The fact that money is there causes traders to bring more goods to the people to extract it. Although competitive consumption is not a big matter at the Coast it is beginning to appear. If wants cannot be satisfied governments face discontent.

The readiest solution is wage labour. While wage labour is physically much harder work than tending one's own field, it has advantages. You are told what to do and, if you do it, you get a given amount of money at the end. This is psychologically the easiest way to enter the money economy. Its rewards may be limited but you know precisely what you are getting for your effort. It may seem a lot and, in the early days, domestic servants were the new rich. The farmer, producing for the market, has not only the hazards of the market itself, and he is at a disadvantage *vis à vis* the experienced middleman, but hazards of weather and disease as well. Beside which he has to learn how to farm, be able to put out capital, or to borrow it, and risk ruin. No country has extension services on a scale that will fully protect the farmer. Again, there is a great inertia to be overcome in moving the farmer from subsistence agriculture to production for the market. If, from his subsistence-farming position, he sees the wage labourer becoming relatively 'rich', he can do likewise and leave his wife to look after the subsistence-farming, which is her traditional job, anyway, and seek work. As population grows, however slowly, and as consumption competition increases, however slowly (and his wife will no doubt ask him for a new skirt like her neighbour's) he will help to swell the number of wage-seekers and of the apparent unemployed. If he does this he then becomes a statistical and (I was about to add 'therefore') real problem for the government, He may, before entering the labour market, have represented hidden underemployment on the land, but his departure has not enabled the land to be more productive.

All this could, no doubt, be taken care of, in an initially thinly populated area, by the 'normal' rate of development, whatever that may be. I mean by it a rate which keeps pace with the slow acceleration of all the pressures that I have described. This may beg the question, but it is illustrative. The pressures, at some point, will continue to accelerate at a pace that no rate of economic growth that can be expected in any developing country can match. Demand, whether in the form of necessities or desires, will outrun the ability to supply. This produces an unstable situation for which political outlets may be sought.

The demand for necessities comes from increased population; the demand for other things from envy, keeping-up-with-the-Joneses, and, particularly, from improved communications. Means of communication (not transport) grow slowly at first but their rate of acceleration is the fastest of all. They are used first by those who try to increase production, but they also demonstrate how others live. Governments will argue whether the best way to increase production is not to stimulate consumption. Whichever answer is reached, both will work together. Even if the government does not positively stimulate consumption, sellers of goods will. So will everyone from advanced countries, from politicians to social workers, who express horror at the lamentable conditions in which people live, even though it may be well ahead of that of the masses of Asia.

When demand of whatever kind (and yesterday's luxuries are today's necessities) begins rapidly to outstrip production it presents a problem which is as difficult for a colonial as for an independent government to solve. It has often been suggested that Britain is getting out of Africa at just this point in time in most colonies; the point where the problem becomes insoluble. I shall try to show that there are many other reasons for Britain 'getting out of Africa' and the apparent insolubility of the problem is not one of them. The forces that go to make this problem, however, also create a number of other pressures that contribute to the reasons for getting out.

Development does not accelerate steadily. It goes by fits and starts. This produces, beside the basic disequilibrium, a succession of disequilibria. These produce hardship, disappointment of expectation, social upsets (how has that socially insignificant fellow become richer and more important than I, who am older and have a higher traditional status?). These, in turn, tend to seek political outlets, or become the fodder of politicians. It is sufficient to note, at this stage, that economic development, because it never keeps pace with social change, produces, not only social disequilibria, but a disequilibrium in individuals, particularly when development is not part of the *mores* of the people. A bewildered and unhappy people results. This no doubt contributes to the particular nature of African politics although, in truth, they differ more in their manifestations than otherwise from European politics.

The Coast hinterland

The combination of development at the Coast and the beginnings of a changed outlook affected not only the peoples of the Coastal Strip but those of the Coast hinterland as well. The hinterland is poor country with little rain and gives way within a short distance to the arid, semi-desert areas between Mombasa and Nairobi, given over to national parks (game reserves) except for some sisal plantations in the shadow of the Teita Hills and the Hills themselves, about 100 miles inland. The people in the hinterland, attracted by the magnet of possible employment at the Coast and persuaded by two years of exceptional drought in 1959–60, moved down into the Coastal Strip, squatted on land wherever there was any available or sought employment. This increased the pressure on the Strip and created a situation which could be used politically. The Coast was faced with the problem of finding employment at a rate beyond that at which it was growing, in spite of having, in Mombasa, the second town in Kenya, the major port of East Africa and a small industrial complex. The difficulty was increased because the growth rate of Mombasa was reduced after the first independence talks in 1960. When the drought was over those that had moved into the Coastal Strip did not return to the hinterland, if indeed they could then have got land there. Beyond the hope of employment, even if it became unemployment, and beyond the squatted-on lands, there were new delights, cinemas, town life, but above all freedom from tribal custom. The pull of the city is not only its material attractions but its freedom. In the towns a new African grows up, one not divorced from the tribe entirely but turning his back on it.

The value of this consideration of the Coast is that it has enabled us to see some of the natural effects of economic change, which underlie movements in other parts of the country. The description can easily give an exaggerated impression of how things go, and at the Coast they go more gently than elsewhere. The only thing peculiar to the Coast was the drought in the hinterland which accelerated a natural process. What is happening there is common to all underdeveloped countries and we can see the forces of change at work. At *uhuru* we see economic change beginning to produce disequilibria between economic and social change, the inertia of agriculture and a growing unemployment problem. None of these were of desperate proportions. Tensions were growing and we shall see later what happened. These movements, however, do not necessitate independence, are not a cause but a condition of it. In other parts of the country the rate of change has been both quicker and slower according to local conditions. The Coast was not a part of the 'white highlands' but is important because of its similarity in structure to Zanzibar and the Tanganyika Coast. In Kenya, however, the centre of affairs is not at the Coast but inland, and one would not expect the pattern of its neighbours to be followed.

The Teita Hills

A hundred miles from the Coast rise the Teita Hills, a massive block rising out of the dry plains, at the top of which in rich, well-watered, broken country, some 5,000 families live. The people are interesting because they show the most diverse physical types. It seems that the hills have been a place of refuge for those fleeing from slave raiders, tribal wars, etc. Except for a number of sisal estates, now largely Asian-owned, in the rain shadow of the hills, at Voi and Taveta, the arid plains surround the hills on all sides. The people of the hills need not detain us beyond noting some general problems that they exemplify, particularly the severe limits to their terrain and what this means in relation to population growth. They have no outlets of more land beyond what can be irrigated in the plains below. Water is not plentiful for irrigation and irrigation itself is expensive. It needs high-priced cash crops to maintain it, leaving aside the recovery of its capital cost. Cash crops depend on a market and the nearest is Mombasa, where the products of the Teita have to compete with those of the Coastal Strip and at prices net of heavy transport costs. While, therefore, in most of the highlands of Kenya it is possible to cause intensified agricultural development and to bring agriculture into the money economy, thus absorbing more people on the land, there are severe limitations to this here. Nor are there nearby uses for labour. The economy of the Teita must always have a large subsistence element since the cost of importing food to the hills is high. Transport costs for an island surrounded by land are very much higher than for one surrounded by water. The Teita themselves have in miniature, a problem that Kenya has as a whole, the disparity of export and import costs. We shall look more closely at this later. The general position of the Teita is that they must export labour permanently to more distant places as their population grows. Although otherwise like the Kenya highlands they have a more intractable problem which is not, at the moment, acute. Some tension is beginning to develop but they are hard put to find real political grievances, as we shall see. They have identified themselves with the Kikuyu–Luo axis politically, presumably because they are land-hungry but do not fear territorial expansion by the Kikuyu.

At least the Teita can seek employment elsewhere, even if there is little available. No national borders prevent their migration. In this they are more fortunate than under-developed countries as a whole. The advanced countries of the world can, by mass production methods, produce consumer goods at a much cheaper price than they can be produced locally. If we take clothing as an example, and assume a backward country which had, nevertheless, been accustomed to wear clothes and to make them (and there are plenty of such in the world), the country will now buy these products from abroad and its own spinners, weavers, cobblers will be put out of work. This is possible because the country is producing primary raw materials for the advanced country instead, and spinners, weavers and cobblers can, in theory, become coffee or tea growers instead, although there are practical difficulties. Disequilibria and tensions are caused in bringing this about. It assumes, too, that there is unlimited demand for coffee and tea and unlimited land to grow them on. This is far from being the case. If the spinners, weavers and cobblers could move to the places where the mass production factories are situated the problem would be resolved. This is not permitted and the rich countries protect their new wealth from those that they have thrown out of work elsewhere. Clearly this situation is masked in a country such as Kenya, where there were no spinners, weavers or cobblers, but there were potential ones. The lack of mobility of labour serves to impoverish the growing populations of the poorer countries. In time this could right itself by increasing variety of development in the poor countries and the growth of their internal market, but this is a long haul.[1]

[1] It is true, of course, that imports of cheap consumer goods have to be paid for, and to do this foreign exchange must be earned through increased exports, so that, in theory, there must be more employment in the export industries. But any *developing* country must have an adverse balance of visible trade, which means that there is an inflow of capital, in one form or another, which in turn will be spent on consumer as well as capital goods. The local spinner, weaver and cobbler cannot compete with cheap imports and there will be structural difficulties in the local economy which will prevent him transferring to the export sector (limitations on the acquisition of land, existing overpopulation in the agricultural areas, apart from a tendency of governments, particularly

They are generally prevented from taking advantage of their main asset, poverty and cheapness of labour, and exporting manufactures to advanced countries and, in any case, the pattern of trade, primary agricultural products in return for manufactures, hinders them from acquiring manufacturing skills. As we shall see later, Kenya was in a special position, pre-independence, to make a break-through in this problem. The Teita have enabled us to be introduced to it.

THE PASTORAL TRIBES

The pastoral tribes occupying the semi-arid areas of the north of Kenya do not, with one exception, present any special problems. They are, more than the settled tribes, addicted and adapted to a particular mode of life which is not easily susceptible of change. They have not changed. The only significant change would be for them to abandon their way of life and become settled agriculturalists. Over most of the area this is not possible. The exception, the Somalis of the north-east, are a minor irritant. They want to be associated politically with their kinsmen in Somalia and do not want to be ruled by 'Africans'.

This cannot be allowed because all African countries realize that the old colonial boundaries, however arbitrary and irrational, must be maintained—partly because they are irrational. If not, all governments would be suspect. Colonial boundaries paid only a limited regard to tribal boundaries and most African countries have tribes whose lands lie across their borders. If claims for tribal unity and self-determination were accepted the map of Africa would dissolve. The word 'tribe' itself has almost become a dirty

---

under foreign impulses, to seek to increase agricultural efficiency in terms of man-power rather than acreage). The same applies, with more force, to the inadequately developing country, with a surplus on visible trade.

word in political language. To accept the principle of tribal self-determination would strengthen every fissiparous tendency and every sectional leader in countries that are desperately striving for unity. This was the argument against Mr Tshombe, that he threatened to break up the sacred boundaries of the Congo. (The argument for him is that the Congo was too big and too little unified to be an effective country.) The African leaders know the danger of the tribal problem and this has spurred them on to talk of regional federations and Pan-African unity. In so far as they are successful in inspiring and constructing national unity, so the tribe will become less important and, with it, the urgency for federations, etc. Particularly will this be so as the new governments get control of greater physical force.

The pastoral tribes, then, maintain an ancient way of life and nature preserves their population balance in its ancient way. Droughts and floods may upset this balance, and used to cause colonial governments worry. Neither the areas nor the peoples have a potential for economic development.[1]

The Masai, situated on both sides of the southern border of Kenya, present particular features. An inward-looking group, they have usually strenuously resisted any attempts at development. They would like improved water supplies, but that is all. A recent proposal to develop a 200,000 acre ranch for them was turned down, with the warning that anyone who went near the area would have a spear in his back. They have in their possession 1,400,000 acres of good agricultural land which they rarely use, even for grazing. It is rather higher and colder than they like. Nor will they let anyone else use it. This is a potential source of trouble in a country where so many are land-hungry or, simply, hungry. At present attention is diverted from this to the European

---

[1] Minor improvement is possible. The Hides and Skins Improvement Service was able, in a few years, to double the value of the exports of hides and skins without increasing the quantity.

lands. The general public wants the European farms which they know well and which are within their tribal 'spheres of influence'. They would not easily be diverted to the Masai lands which they do not know and which are far from their tribal homelands. To try to settle these lands would cause trouble for the government with the Masai where no trouble now exists.

THE HIGHLANDS

We can now turn to the heart of Kenya, the highlands, and particularly to the 'land question'. The expression 'highlands' does not mean the 'white highlands'. For that will be used the current, and almost synonymous, expression 'the scheduled areas'. These were the areas scheduled under the Agriculture Ordinance to which guaranteed minimum returns on the planting of certain crops applied.

Here we return to our 'fifths'. Of the rich lands of Kenya only one-fifth was in European hands and of the European lands only one-fifth was rich land. The highlands are mountainous, broken country, of great variety, lying above 5,000 feet and cultivable up to 9,000 feet. At the turn of the century, when Europeans came to Kenya, the highlands consisted of certain blocks of rich land lying on the well-watered slopes of the mountains with larger and drier stretches of flatter land lying in between. To the west lay the Lake Victoria basin, the most densely populated part of the country, running from the slopes of Mt Elgon and the hills surrounding the lake down to the lake shore. It was inhabited by the Luo on the shore and to the south and by the Abaluhya tribes to the north. Here there are now densities of 1,400–1,600 per square mile. To the east on the slopes of the Aberdare Mountains (in the rain shadow) and on the slopes of Mount Kenya lay the densely populated Kikuyu tribe, with lesser densities to the east and south-east of

Mount Kenya occupied by the Meru and Embu. In between these two blocks is the Rift Valley, stretching away into the deserts of the north, an area then roamed by the Masai pastoralists. The lands ranged by the Masai were generally poorer, from purely ranching lands to some areas suitable for mixed farming.

In exploring the origins of *uhuru*, of the creation of an African State in this particular part of the world, it is necessary, for a complete picture, to consider briefly how Kenya came into being at all. The opening-up of East Africa represented one of the last urges of the European expansion of the nineteenth century. This expansion was made possible by the railway. Earlier European expansion had been coastal except in India, with only limited penetration inland. The railway provided an instrument for opening up the interior and for reaching new resources and new wealth. It had already pushed the frontiers of the United States and Canada across the North American continent to the Pacific and had caught the imagination of all. Here was a fruitful tool for developing the backward areas of the world and for bringing their riches to the West in return for what the West could give. It would revolutionize the world—and did. Only the West could give the railways but all would benefit. So, of course, would the railway promoters. Railways needed the support of civil authority. There must be peace and internal security if railways were to flourish and perform their task. They required order as much as the expansion of shipping had required freedom from piracy. So railway advance and European administration went hand in hand, in Southern Africa, in East Africa, even in Russian Asia. The railway and the steam locomotive were transforming the face of the world. They had made the rapid development of Europe possible and railway entrepreneurs were seeking new worlds to conquer. It was a venture for which capital was readily available, nor did governments hesitate to put their own finances into railways. At the turn of the century the fashionableness of railway-building had not been seriously challenged by the internal combustion engine. It was the thing to do. It is instructive, as I have pointed out in *The Pattern of a Dependent Economy*,[1] to read the debates of the Legislative Council of British Honduras, a small country of 50,000 inhabitants, at that time. The legislators were caught by the railway fever and were determined to have a railway. The argument was about where it should go. This fashionableness did not disappear until the first world war.

So a railway, and with it European administration, came to East Africa. It set in train a series of events which were to issue in an independent Kenya and its effect is far from exhausted. Its necessities determined the structure of the country. At first it was the more advanced Uganda that was expected to make the railway pay, but it was quickly realized that freight would have to be found within the 600 miles that it ran from Uganda to the sea, especially as it only reached Uganda in its last stage. By that time the idea of European settlement in Uganda had been disposed of. It was observed that some of the land through which the railway ran in Kenya was capable of agricultural development. Quick development was needed. This could only be achieved by bringing in European settlers. At the same time the building of the railway itself required the importation of trained labour and craftsmen. These were to be found most readily in India. They were followed by Indian traders.

European settlement was not confined, as it largely was in Northern Rhodesia, to a narrow strip on either side of the railway line. It spread wider and branch lines were constructed for it. Settlement occurred mainly in parts of the areas ranged by the Masai suitable for agriculture or ranching. Various arrangements were made with the Masai by treaty

[1] C.U.P., 1953.

c

by which they surrendered these lands and moved south to their present position (where the treaties guaranteed them perpetual security and protection). Settlement also took place in certain empty lands between various hostile tribes. These were really no-man's-lands where there was no cultivation because of disputed tribal title to the land and tribal warfare. Examples are to be found in the Sotik area (between the Kisii and the Kipsigis) and in the Miwani area (between the Luo, the Nandi and the Kipsigis). This latter was the only area where Asian settlement was allowed; it was below the altitude used for the early rough definitions of the 'white highlands'. It is interesting to note that the Indian government in imperial times exerted continual pressure on the Kenya administration in the interests of Asians in Kenya. None of this settlement seems to have caused great heart-burning, probably because the tribes concerned were not pressed for land, and are still not pressed, with the exception of the Luo, whose claim to European land is, anyway, small and strongly disputed by other tribes.

Settlement also took place near Nairobi, on the Masai-Kikuyu borderlands, in rich agricultural land claimed by the Kikuyu. It was temporarily unoccupied for two reasons. The Kikuyu numbers appear to have been reduced at that time by disease. The practice of shifting cultivation left large areas unoccupied which were really lying fallow and regenerating after a period of cultivation. Some settlement also took place in the area with Kikuyu consent and by purchase, but with the usual misunderstanding which arises when land is the subject of transactions between parties with completely different concepts of land law. The European understood that he was acquiring freehold. This concept was unknown to the Kikuyu (although they themselves purchased land from the more primitive hunting peoples of the forests). Land was held by the tribe only, although they were accustomed to the idea of having *ahoy*, or tenants-at-will, within their system. They seem to have regarded the European settlers in this light, since it was unthinkable to them that the land of the tribe could be permanently alienated. As the numbers of the Kikuyu grew again this became a source of bitter anti-European feeling. Even though their claims were investigated in great detail by the Carter Commission in the 1930s and compensatory boundary adjustments made, the feelings engendered were not assuaged. The Kikuyu think that the Europeans stole their land by a trick and, by extension, that the Europeans stole all the African land they hold. The European lands to the north of Nairobi are rich lands and the generally more developed state of European farms gives the impression that European land is richer than African, although four-fifths of the rich land remained in African hands. The great bulk of the European lands are relatively poorer and would yield little under subsistence agriculture. It is important, however, in relation to the history of Kenya, to note this special position of the Kikuyu and the demonstration-effect of European agricultural development. It will be noted, too, how the Kikuyu extend their own situation to the whole of Kenya. Similarly the Mau Mau has been extended to become the Kenya Freedom Movement.[1]

The importance of land in the Kenya scene cannot be exaggerated. It gives rise to more emotion than any other subject, even though the emotion may be expressed in other forms. Europeans also show emotion over it although it is of less significance for them. For Africans the ownership of land is the only social security that they know. A few acres can ensure a livelihood and the indigenous social systems revolve around land-ownership. Traditionally, everyone in the tribe can obtain land from the tribe. Tensions rise high

[1] This account of European settlement is based on a paper by Professor W. T. W. Morgan, 'The White Highlands of Kenya', *The Geographical Journal*, vol. 129, part 2, June 1963.

when the tribe can no longer fulfil this responsibility. The tribal structure begins to disintegrate under the strain, and new forces and conflicts are let loose. It is at this point, when the tribe can no longer fulfil its duty to its members, that we look for the most intense political activity—and where we find it; where we look for an understanding of political alignments—and find the land-hungry tribes in one group and the rest in another.

The social security aspect of land continues under economic farming. Traditionally women grow the family food supply. This continues even when the man is now producing for the market. The wife (or wives) must have her (their) food plot(s). In the past this system has released the man for wage-earning (and enabled employers to pay a single wage instead of a family wage). Now it provides a basic security for the economic farmer. European farmers have followed the custom and given their labourers their own subsistence plots. African farmers who employ labourers tend to do the same. With this basic security established the demand for money wages is less.

Particularly is land the interest of the tribe. The land belongs to it and all land in Kenya could be regarded as 'belonging' (in a broad sense) to one tribe or another.[1] The Masai formally surrendered their claims over large areas (claims which were only disputed at their edges). Other tribes did not. Land is not only a personal matter of great importance but a tribal matter of great importance as well. Even the tribes which were not pressed for land and tolerated the Europeans would be angered at the thought of Africans of another tribe occupying land which they regarded as theirs. When the over-riding European power is removed, large emotional forces are released. The idea that everyone is entitled to have land from the tribe is still paramount. The acceptance of other means of livelihood is still

[1] Except in the Coastal Strip with its long history of Arab rule.

basically an alien idea, although circumstances will gradually compel new attitudes, or at least the acceptance of the realities of life. This belief in the right of every man to land is transferred to the idea of independence, especially among those tribes which can no longer provide for every member from their own tribal lands. At independence all will be given land. The tribes with plenty of land are worried and hasten to secure their own tribal lands from being given to others. They are natural allies of the Europeans but, if the European is to go, then they must protect themselves.

The advent of Europeans, however, in the beginning, had settled inter-tribal land quarrels. Two large concentrations of African population were left to the east and west of the highlands—Europeans settled in between. In the two dense African areas, the stabilization of boundaries and the removal of natural checks on population growth, caused acute disequilibria and steadily growing pressures within a limited space.

The history of the development of Kenya is for the greater part of its course the history of European development. Development meant the development of agriculture, as there were only negligible mineral and fuel resources in Kenya. The development of African agriculture offered little promise.

The early years of settlement were given over to experimenting with what could be done with the land. It was not until the second world war that development became positive and planned. Previously planned development had not been one of the accepted ideas. Development was regarded as an individual problem. Planning received considerable impetus from socialist thinking and from the achievements of the Soviet Union. It was further spurred on by the depression of the 1930s. In any case, communications and transport were only slowly growing in the pre-war period, while research and experiment were still exiguous. The effects of the depression itself caused the beginning of the organization of the economy. A number of statutory organizations were set up to defend the economy rather than promote it.

The pattern of development was the cultivation of coffee and tea on the richer lands, the ranching of beef and dairy cattle and sheep on the poorer lands, the growing of sisal on the drier good land, with mixed farming (dairy cattle, wheat, maize, barley and pyrethrum) on the remainder.

The war and the need to supply the allied forces centred on East Africa with their basic foodstuffs gave an immense impetus to mixed farming. It caused the government to intervene actively in the promotion of an agriculture that would supply, and quickly, the army's needs and those of the population of East Africa as a whole, particularly the towns and estates. A drought and maize famine in 1942 had emphasized the need for regulatory machinery, stabilizing measures and inducements. The organizations then set up demonstrated clearly how much could be achieved by organized development in the protected war-time market, but also prevented the situation from being exploited. After the war the high prices ruling continued to give a favourable impetus to development and this was extended by the Korean war boom. It would be some time before Kenya had to chase falling prices with increased production. Kenya emerged from the war with its economy strengthened and a great deal of knowledge of how to organize production, and of skill in doing so. Meanwhile its internal economy was expanding.

The war brought to East Africa many who would otherwise not have been aware of it. They saw opportunities for themselves. Many were demobilized there (or moved into Kenya later on the demise of the 'groundnuts scheme' in Tanganyika). They set up small businesses and industries or supplied skills and executive abilities which were needed. They were of a different kind from the old settlers—

essentially townsmen who would not normally have thought of emigration. A new influx of farming settlers also occurred, with positive aid from the government in strengthening the new European country in Africa. The European Agricultural Settlement Board was set up with government funds and assisted new farming immigrants while many, with capital, came of their own accord. The Board was still bringing in immigrants, with the assistance of British funds, as late as 1960. (By 'British funds' I mean this: the Kenya budget was underpinned by British assistance, and budget uses, especially those that were not straightforward administrative costs, had to be specifically approved by Britain when the measure of assistance was negotiated.) The new immigrants came to a freedom from customary restraints in Britain (compare the attraction of the Coast for the people of the Coast hinterland and the attractions of cities everywhere in offering freedom from tribal restraints) to a country of opportunity (and many were pure opportunists).

With the immigrants came capital and more followed. The post-war years showed a continual and heavy net capital inflow, even during the Mau Mau Emergency when the image of the land of opportunity was barely dimmed. Kenya sustained for years a heavy deficit on the visible balance of trade as development went ahead. Part of this was paid for by the tourist trade and part by invisible exports of commercial services to the rest of East Africa as Nairobi became the commercial centre of an area far beyond the borders of Kenya and particularly within the East African common market. It would, however, be true to say that any enterprise with any reasonable prospect of success, on any scale, could find the capital.[1]

This development was aided by a positive development

[1] There was also an influx of funds connected with the presence of British troops during the Mau Mau Emergency, increased later by the establishment of a British military base.

programme and a highly organized marketing structure for agriculture, the base of the economy, while small entre-preneurs experimented with new activities with a freedom that they would have had difficulty in finding in Britain. They were assisted by the town planners and the railways in the preparation of well-served industrial sites. The post-war government in Britain gave a positive impulse to planned development. Every colony was required to produce its development plan. All circumstances conspired to accelerate the rate of economic change, so that any strains set up by disequilibria between social and economic change were accentuated. Nor were the effects confined to Europeans. Growth spilled over among Africans, particularly increasing the numbers in paid employment and offering them new opportunities for work. The effects on the social structure were not obvious at the time. In so far as African economic development was concerned it was simply regarded as good. The labour-absorptive powers of development relieved some of the problems of the African areas and masked the social problems. The effect of economic development in a society geared to thinking in its terms was, however, very different from its effect on a society geared to think in different terms. Thus the post-war attitude to development did much in it-self to create an unstable country. Nor is this instability re-moved by independence.

It is worth looking at some of the positive development measures which contributed to this progress since we shall later be considering both whether they are likely to continue to function and also whether the growth rate, interrupted by the independence talks, can be renewed. Although these measures were primarily directed at the European sector, many of them were effective to a greater or lesser degree in the African sector.

The positive measures for agricultural development were the creation of widespread extension services and a network of specialized research stations and generalized experimental stations of a high standard and of national value. No under-developed country had a staffing ratio to agricultural popula-tion (even in the African areas) comparable with this. Coupled with it was a farm planning service and a soil con-servation service. These were able to pursue increased pro-ductivity. The European settlers responded in varying degrees, but on the whole set about developing their farms on a long-term plan, ploughing back their profits each year. Those with more capital or better land advanced most rapidly; those with least most slowly. Apart from the rich and well-developed tea and coffee estates it would be fair to say that on the average the European farmers were in mid-development when the independence talks began, with their resources ploughed back into the land and probably another 10–20 years before the results of their efforts reached full fruition. In furthering this progress the government assisted by long-term supervised credit tied to an approved farm development plan.

The development of the marketing structure came from the lessons learnt first during the depression and then during the war. There was soon erected a structure which was only equalled in complexity and effectiveness by European countries. The forms of the structure, as applied to different products, were varied, but their underlying principles were the same. They sought stability in agriculture and the control of markets. These are worth looking at in more detail since they are often misunderstood by economists who have a doctrinaire attachment to free enterprise based on highly theoretical and abstract models which do not exist anywhere in reality and which ignore the international immobility of labour, and whose thinking is too often an attempt to apply to agriculture what are basically industrial models, and since we shall later be assessing how far the organization of agri-culture is really possible in under-developed countries.

The farmer is faced by exceptional hazards over which he has no control and which he cannot forecast; the market price of his output, either local or for export, the weather and disease. The industrialist operates in a more stable environment and the changes in that environment caused by competition, new ideas and new methods, take place more slowly and give him time to adapt. One can well imagine the brake on investment in industry that would be caused if the industrialist did not know whether the weather might not double or halve his production, or whether disease might not attack his products. Obviously there are great risks in industry but they are calculable and the industrialist takes, as the saying goes, 'a calculated risk'. The farmer's risks, in a completely free society, are incalculable and every advanced country in the world does all it can to make them more calculable. Organized marketing removes one of the hazards (research assists with the others) so that he can make long-term plans with more confidence. The essence of agricultural development is land improvement and this requires planning far ahead. This is a common problem for all races. One of the big hindrances to African agricultural development has been the inability of the farmer, because of the land-tenure system, to do so. Similarly it prevents governments making long-term plans for agricultural development. Too much government planning of agriculture is no more than a generalization of statistics; if a country uses so much more fertilizer or so many more tractors it should produce so much more; let us therefore produce so much more fertilizer and so many more tractors and, hey presto, agricultural production will rise. This is the industrialist approach to agriculture; the application of the relatively simple and measurable problems of the factory to the farm. During the war and for some time afterwards under-developed countries sold their produce overseas on long-term contracts, and this was immensely valuable as it enabled them to make long-term plans instead of having to take a series of emergency measures as prices fluctuated. With the disappearance of these contracts a substitute is necessary. We have already noted the need for a large price incentive to persuade the subsistence farmer to transfer his efforts (or to make the effort) to production for the market. Much of Africa is not producing what it could or supporting the population that it could because the incentive to do so is lacking.[1] Marketing organizations, by cutting out the middleman, enable a greater part of the retail price to be returned to the farmer and the incentive to produce is increased. Organized marketing cannot, of course, eliminate the middleman's real costs, although it can rationalize the movement of produce and save transport costs. The real objection to the middleman is not his true costs but his speculative costs. These are real enough to him. He has to make guesses about demand and supply over a large area (which may include overseas markets) and he must, in his price to the producer, protect himself against unknowns and the market going against him. He does this by offering the farmer the lowest price he can. He may be a trader as well and know that he will sell more trade goods if he pays more for produce, but the risks on produce trading will be much greater than on the selling of consumer-goods.

Instability stifles agricultural initiative in the individual and in the state, yet agricultural development and efficiency offer the most rapid possibilities of increasing wealth in underdeveloped societies and have a high capital/output ratio, partly because they are starting from nothing and two factors of production, land and labour, are plentiful and cheap. The problem is to provide encouraging circumstances for capital.

The economic problems of agricultural development are particularly well-exemplified in Kenya, where the heart of

[1] Ester Boserup, in her brilliant *Conditions of Agricultural Growth* (Allen & Unwin, 1965), brings out clearly this problem of incentives in peasant agriculture.

the country is 300–500 miles from its port. So is its main internal market. This means that its imports are unduly expensive and its exports correspondingly costly. It has a natural, geographical protection against imports and a natural handicap on exports. This is the well-known import/export parity price problem. The import parity price is the price of imports at their source *plus* all the costs of getting them to the Kenya market. The export parity price is the price obtainable in export markets *minus* all the costs of getting them to those markets. This has two basic effects. It means that imports are not available at a price that can stimulate the producer to greater efforts, since they will tend to be beyond his means. On the other hand, exports are limited to those crops that can command a high price on the world's markets. If the price falls, because of over-production in some other part of the world, the product may be not saleable and the farmer is discouraged, if not ruined, since he cannot produce coffee this year and tea next year. With annual crops he has more possibility of change, but not unless they have the same labour and machinery requirements and he has suitable soil. He loses two incentives to production; the consumer-competition stimulus and the stability to enable him to plan ahead. The former can be overcome by the growth of local industries under the protection afforded by distance (and, perhaps, tariffs, although too high tariffs may make the product so expensive that it fails to have the desired consumer effect, reducing the size of the market and its own scope for expansion; nor will competition remedy this since the industry rarely is able to support at the beginning more than one factory of a kind or it will lose the economies of scale). But local industries need local markets first and they too depend on stability and growth in agriculture. So a vicious circle exists which hinders internal growth and limits development.

Leaving aside the problems of industry for the local

market, what of agriculture for the local market? I am not postulating a start from scratch; virgin land and new people, although new people have to be fed. The argument commences with the export of high-priced cash crops. These in turn create an internal market for agricultural products, chiefly foods. Production for this market grows within the natural protection of distance. Prices cannot be higher than the cost of imports plus freight plus any tariff, but are unlikely to be much lower. This provides a good stimulus to production in a limited and slowly growing market. As agriculture develops and communications improve (and both do so irregularly; in certain crops in the case of the former; in certain areas in the case of the latter) it is not long before a number of farmers producing independently supply the available local market. (The definition of 'local market' can include places beyond the borders of Kenya when Kenya goods are competitive under a similar protection of distance; the size of the local market can be expanded if transport costs can be reduced, but this depends on growth in the bulk to be carried.) The farmers, at that point, may overproduce, but whatever else happens their further efforts are limited to the small local market although their potential production at that price (or at a lower price) may be greater. Whether they overproduce or underproduce for this market is not in their own hands. It may be decided by the weather. Nor can it be nicely calculated, even if this did not affect it, since a multitude of farmers will not be aware of the point when a surplus will appear. What happens at this point to the price? Once there is a surplus it must be stored or exported. On our assumptions there will be no storage, nor can all products be stored indefinitely. Storage, anyway, costs money. The price obtainable for export is the price in the foreign market less freight and less any tariff at the other end. There is then a wide difference between the import price and the net export price. The price offered to farmers by middlemen will be governed by the net export price. Middlemen may be able, perhaps, not to buy all the crop at export parity (which may itself be fluctuating) but in a situation of uncertainty about what can be obtained, and one where the trade passes through a chain of middlemen, the tendency will be for export parity in any part of the country to decide the price that the farmer gets. This may benefit the consumer but it inhibits production and thereby the expansion of agriculture, the only available resource, and the growth of a rural market on which local industry can be based. Next year the farmer, if he is able to switch, ceases to produce that crop and the price rises again. Violent price fluctuations follow, unless the farmer drops out altogether. A situation is created in which he cannot plan long-term investment in the improvement of his land and his productivity. This is what happened in Tanganyika and Uganda when they eventually abandoned controlled marketing. It is necessary to control the supply to the local market in a separate compartment from the supply to the export market and to eliminate the middleman effect described above by the handling of marketing by one organization. This organization can then pay to the producer the highest incentive price possible by averaging the prices obtained in the internal market with those obtained for exports. In its export appearance this is technically described by economists as 'dumping'—selling abroad at a price lower than the goods are sold at home. There is hardly a country in the world exporting agricultural products that does not do this, although it may mask it in a variety of ways. It provides agricultural stability, lessens price fluctuations, maintains agricultural incomes, spreads them widely and creates a wider consumer market for industry. Because nearly every other country does it it is necessary for an agricultural producer country to protect itself from having it done to it by tariffs, import restrictions, etc.

The logic of the statutory marketing organization is that if its new averaged local and export price is still profitable to the producer, or more profitable than an alternative use of his land, he will continue to produce more and his average price will continue to fall, but not catastrophically in any year, until he can no longer do so. There may be other producers who can. The price will finally settle at a level at which the greatest production is achieved. The industry will then be in the hands of the most efficient producers. The others, if they had grown that crop, will have to find the best alternative use for their land. Maximum production of the crop and maximum spread of the return from it will have been achieved, be it 90 per cent for export or only 10 per cent. This is the theory but, to put it into practice, it needs a firm, principled and knowledgeable administration.

In practice the marketing organizations tend to be managed by the producers themselves, although the final say in pricing is with the government and the producers form a strong pressure group. As soon as a price reduction, resulting from increased production causing exports, begins to make production unprofitable for the less efficient producers, remedial action is taken. Either an attempt is made to raise the internal price (this is significant only if the local market takes a large proportion of the whole crop) or, more likely, an attempt is made to restrict the numbers of producers by licensing new entrants into the field, or production quotas are imposed maintaining profitability over a smaller quantity. All these measures are nationally damaging since they restrain development, prolong inefficiency and limit the benefits derived from a particular crop to those who were the first to produce it. New entrants are excluded. This has a special importance in Kenya because Europeans were in all cases the first producers and the marketing organizations tended to preserve their position.

Organized marketing can take a variety of forms in

practice. A co-operative trying to perform the functions outlined (and not merely a subsidiary in the marketing process) will generally need state legal support. It will create a stable market through its monopoly, will direct producers where and how to sell (and no one really enjoys being organized in this way) and will provide stable prices. By so doing it produces particular and local market disequilibria in which individual members of the co-operative can see an advantage to themselves in avoiding the organization. This applies, too, to the statutory organization. While, therefore, statutory (or co-operative) marketing will be in the *general* interest of producers, it will frequently run counter to what individuals regard as their *particular* interests. Statutory organizations are, therefore, continually subject to attack and their position weakened by 'black marketing'. This is a classic example of the contrast between Rousseau's 'general will' and 'the will of all'.

It has been necessary to consider this matter at length for two reasons. While the arguments for this essential tool of development are well-known to American and continental economists, British economists seem unfamiliar with them, or unconvinced, or not wanting to be convinced. In the second place, Kenya has been equipped with such a tool and it has played a large part in its development, in a wide variety of organizations adapted to the particular crops that they handle. This is the great gift of the colonial administration and the European settler to *uhuru* in Kenya. We shall have to wonder whether the tool can still be used after independence, knowing that it demands sound and capable administration and skill in its use, and that it is a tool that by its nature provokes hostility and opposition among those who do not understand its principles. It is a tool of freedom to those who accept it but a tool of oppressive restriction to those who do not.

So equipped, the Kenya European farmer had supplied

the armies in East Africa during the war, as well as the towns and estate labour of East Africa, with their bread, butter, milk and meat. As the wartime organizations were dismantled they were replaced (but not in Uganda and Tanganyika) by others, and Kenya continued to supply East Africa and was beginning to feel out for new markets in the Indian Ocean area, such as the growing oil centres of the Persian Gulf. Here it was hindered by the fact that shipping routes ran to and from Europe and not across the Indian Ocean. It was only a matter of time before the investment in new shipping routes would become as important as the investment in railways had been. Kenya salesmen were visiting Aden, Bahrein, Kuwait and other places which did not have the same export parity price disadvantages as Europe, although they tended to make up for the lesser distance in higher freight rates and the lack of shipping over the shorter routes.

We have noted how both Tanganyika and Uganda, with whom Kenya shares a common market, made a rather doctrinaire dash for freedom after the wartime marketing organizations were dismantled.[1] This resulted in widespread price fluctuations and a rather chaotic economy in those countries, with much greater difficulty in planning agricultural development. Both have shown signs of wanting to restore organized marketing but they no longer have the machinery and experience to do so. Their first reaction, however, to their self-created difficulties was to blame Kenya for exploiting them. They tried to destroy the common market. They accused Kenya of using common market tariffs and its own controlled marketing to extract the highest prices from them.

[1] Under the influence of the East Africa Royal Commission Report (H.M.S.O. (Cmd. 9475), 1965), sometimes labelled 'the pure milk of Adam Smith'.

D

They received sympathetic attention from a World Bank Economic Survey of Uganda in 1960, and the Raisman Commission in 1961 enquired into this and kindred matters. Kenya had little difficulty in demonstrating that, allowing for day-to-day fluctuations in import parity prices, it sold its produce to East Africa (with one exception) below the import parity price *before* adding customs duty and in arguing further that, if Kenya were compelled to dismantle its marketing structure, production would fall and that Tanganyika and Uganda could not replace it but would have to pay the full import parity price (plus the revenue duty) for the same thing. If this happened the Kenya market for Uganda and Tanganyika products would shrink and with it the local East African market for industry. It is only fair to add that Raisman's colleagues (two well-known British economists) remained unconvinced, even by fact.

The common market is another valuable legacy of the colonial administration, and an instrument for co-ordinating the development of all three countries. To go forward in time, for a moment, it is worth noting that since independence, in spite of interlocking common market constitutional arrangements, there has been less detailed working together than ever before, and each country is pursuing its own economic policies without any regard for the others. The common market as an instrument for common development is fading into a simple customs union and one may well doubt whether, with mutually conflicting policies in all three of its constituent members, it can continue to exist even in that form.

There grew up, then, in the post-war period, a considerable apparatus for developing European agriculture. With these aids, the importation of capital, the ploughing back of profits, and the long- and short-term credit facilities provided by the government, European agriculture did develop.

Much of the effort went into the development of land that was by no means the best in Kenya, although it began to look so and to look, indeed, more developed than it actually was. The farming was fairly large-scale (farms averaging 800–1,000 acres, although the range was 20–40,000), using modern machinery. A farm plan for such a farm is designed to maximize profit for the owner, not simply to maximize total production. What may be a soundly planned farm for this purpose may be capable of greater production (and employment) if farmed differently. The full use of all the land on a farm might involve the outlay of capital on machinery which could not be fully utilized, or a disproportionately high labour force, at certain times only, which might not be readily available. The return on the additional outlay in capital or direct expenditure might be small and put a disproportionate burden on the farmer or his manager and require management time that was not available without increasing overheads. The object of the farm plan is productivity per man not productivity per acre. This will be important for later arguments that arose.

In fact European farmers were large employers of labour. Labour was cheap in money terms: 30s. to 40s. a month. Even in 'real' terms it was not so expensive. The Resident Labourer system enabled the farmer to allocate a portion of his land to each of his labourers for growing their own food supplies. (Any surplus produce the labourer was required to sell through the farmer, but this was for administrative convenience in the marketing system only.) This enabled the African labourer virtually to settle on the farm. Many lived the greater part of their lives on one farm, and many were born and grew up there. The farmer generally supplied medical attention and schooling free. His farm was not at the intensive stage of development so that he did not miss the land so allocated. The numbers that he employed were related to the degree of development. (This statement is relative to the quality of the land; poor land may be relatively more developed and therefore employ 'more', when the actual numbers employed on an undeveloped farm of the same size on good land are greater.) The relation between the numbers employed, or engaged, on the land and the capital employed in developing it is an important factor in relation to arguments about the unemployment problem, collective farms, etc. It would probably be true to say that under European ownership, even allowing for the aim of profitability per owner, the land absorbed as many persons as it could economically at the stage of development reached on any farm. For more to be absorbed more capital was required. The farm also absorbed more than it could absorb under subsistence farming. European farmers then, by their enterprise, had found occupation and a livelihood on the land for more than could have done so before. The land was in the hands of those who could make it productive. In this way a considerable contribution was made by European farm development to absorbing some of the population increase, although there remained a large hidden quantity, in the African lands, of semi-employed.

The labourer population came, in the north, from the overcrowded Abaluhya tribes and, in the south, from the Kikuyu. These, together with Luo, provided the bulk of the working population in the towns.

The development of European farming did much to mitigate the tensions arising from economic disequilibria and population growth, but its *rate* of expansion became slower as growth proceeded. A growth from one to two is a 100 per cent rate, from two to three a 50 per cent rate, and so on. Population growth, however, tends to maintain its rate. In theory agricultural growth might have been quicker if it had been in the hands of African small-holders (on the right kind of land) developing intensively, *if* they knew how to farm; *if* they could get the capital; *if* there were more instructors;

if the land tenure system were different; and many other large ifs and ans that were not satisfied. The point is that European development contributed to stability up to a certain point in time but not thereafter. This point is different in different areas depending on the degree of over-population and the rate of population growth in the adjoining African areas—always remembering that over-population is a relative concept, related to the stage of development reached in those areas. To the Kikuyu areas it ceased to contribute at an early date. To some areas it is still contributing. Which can be seen from the degree of racial tension existing in different areas.

Meanwhile a minor industrial complex was growing up at Nairobi and its satellite Thika, and also at Mombasa. Well-served trading sites were established. Capital flowed in readily from abroad. Men came with their own capital. The attractive climate and congenial way of life lured them. As more industries were established so more came and they could service each other. Asian businessmen invested in industry. A large building industry developed and most large British contracting firms had branches in Kenya. Two cement factories were opened. Nairobi quickly grew to a beautiful city of 270,000 inhabitants. This was in spite of a fairly high rate of taxation and few positive inducements to industry, although the Industrial Development Corporation was ready with capital and guarantees. Expansion throve on expansion. More and more labour was employed. There seemed to be no reason why it should stop. The internal market was growing fast, as we shall see. As the economy grew so more foreign capital became interested. The currency board system, under which the Bank of England was Kenya's central bank, a Bank to which Kenya's foreign exchange needs were marginal, enabled the country to avoid the foreign exchange complications that hampered the development of other under-developed countries. These had to make careful decisions as to how they would spend any foreign exchange earned, and interfere with commerce in order to maintain the soundness of their currency. Nairobi became the commercial centre of East Africa and had considerable invisible exports of commercial services to Tanganyika and Uganda. These, together with industrial exports within the East African common market and the tourist industry, enabled it to finance a high import bill, although the balance of payments concealed a fair-sized capital outflow. The situation seemed to be ideally suited for continuous growth although not, perhaps, economic 'take-off'.

While the European economy was progressing, what was happening in the African sector? For a long time the government's efforts had been limited to attempting to improve subsistence agriculture by enforcing soil conservation measures. These meant little to the people who saw no obvious return for effort. Any return could, in any case, be masked by other influences, weather or disease. There was no money income by which returns could be measured. This caused hostility to the government and to the extension officers of the Department of Agriculture which took much to overcome later on. Nevertheless the government had to take steps to prevent hardship and starvation in the African areas, where the soil was steadily being washed away and the population growing. Other measures seemed impracticable then.

Immediately after the war attention was given to improving water supplies, especially in the drier areas. These were obvious measures with obvious results, although their contribution to the economy as a whole was slight. They were really a means of bettering living conditions in the arid areas and enabling these to sustain a slightly higher population. They improved the subsistence of the areas where they were sited.

The problems of agriculture in the richer lands appeared

still to be intractable. Research was, however, going on into economic small-holdings systems, involving exotic dairy cattle, high-priced cash crops and a plot for the wife to grow the family's basic food supplies. Systems were worked out for the differing agriculture regions. The problem was to get them applied. The chief of these was the customary tribal system of land tenure and the fragmentation of holdings. Capital was needed for development but, even if available, the land occupier had no security of tenure which he could pledge for a loan. There was also the problem of incentives, of demonstrating to the farmer that he could make money without leaving his land. Coffee, tea and other tree crops took some years to reach full bearing. The farmer, who had no experience of them had not the money to plant them nor the income from other sources to pay interest on loans until they bore fruit. The extension services were small and the likelihood of these researches having any effect were small. A stage was reached when it was known what could and should be done to develop African agriculture, but the means were lacking, while there was hostility to the Department of Agriculture. Money was not available for extending services or capital to African areas. The Kenya money economy had been built on European development. European taxpayers objected to 'their' money being spent on Africans. In addition they feared competition from African farmers, whose production costs were thought (erroneously) to be negligible, while it was thought that Africans would produce goods of an inferior quality which would damage the reputation that their own products had been earning in export markets. (Kenya refused to buy Mauritius sugar three years ago because of a poor shipment sent ten years earlier, even though it was known that the poor shipment had been sent on the orders of the British government and against the advice of the Mauritius shippers. Consumer memories are long and confidence, once lost, is hard to restore.) In the event this fear also proved erroneous, but only because of the high standard of extension services established.

Meanwhile population pressure had been growing among the Kikuyu, the Luo and the Abaluhya group. This was mitigated to some extent by the ability of the men to leave the land in the care of their wives and earn money in employment elsewhere. Their need to do so varied with the amount of land that they held. All land was owned by the tribe, but individual rights to cultivate which had been acquired were, with the increase in population and the abandonment of shifting cultivation, which increasing population enforced, beginning to take on much of the appearance of freehold. These rights were passed on by inheritance and each son obtained an equal share. This meant ever-diminishing holdings until some were so small that they could not possibly support a family. Beside this the system of inheritance produced great fragmentation of holdings, so that an individual's holding might be scattered over a wide area. A classic example was a holding of seven acres in twenty-seven scattered fragments. Under such conditions, it is not surprising that the work of agricultural advisers brought little result. Many holdings could never be converted into economic farms producing for the market. When the holding was fragmented no co-ordinated farming of the fragments was possible, while some fragments were so far away as not to be worth the trouble of going to. Even if they had holdings that could produce for the market they had no roads by which to get their produce out.

It was beginning to become clear what must be done if the four-fifths of the richest agricultural land in Kenya was to become productive and make a contribution to the economy. The needs were:

(a) to consolidate in one the fragmented holdings in the over-populated areas so that the holdings could be planned and worked as practical units, a task of immense size involving the registration of all individual rights and their re-arrangement by consent;

(b) to give a secure title to the land holdings, so that farmers could make long-term plans and could borrow on the security of their title for both long- and short-term development;

(c) to find the capital for the African farmers, since the commercial banking system, limited to short-term finance anyway, would not operate in these areas in the initial stages until it could be seen that the new idea was working, and the funds of the Land Bank were fully stretched in European development;

(d) to build roads so that the farmer could get his produce to the marketing centres;

(e) to find the money for the consolidation services, the farm planning services, the surveys, the advisory and extension services, etc., to carry the project out.

It seemed an impossible task: the re-planning and laying out anew of the whole countryside. Even in the areas without land pressure all the items except consolidation were necessary. In those it was necessary to survey, enclose and demarcate existing holdings, and it was there that the first moves were made which proved the technical possibilities of economic small-holdings. But these were not the areas where the major problems lay. To obtain the consent of all in an area to a re-distribution of land seemed unlikely. Money was not available from Kenya's own resources, which were fully taken up in developing the European economy. Private capital would not flow into the African lands. The whole idea ran counter to the natural inclinations and customs of the people. What was needed was an agrarian revolution. In the over-crowded areas the increasing distress of the people as they became poorer, and as their soil washed away into the rivers, caused them to cling more tightly to the illusory security of their traditional ways. They became more reluctant to tackle new ideas. In the Kikuyu areas the situation intrinsically offered more hope. Here was a people, the closest to Nairobi, and more affected by European contact, ingenious, industrious, active and already subject to change. They were even acquainted with a sort of individual land ownership. As no new land was available to the tribe their customary tenure was beginning to approach freehold.

On the other hand the increasing sub-division of the land, the increasing general poverty, the belief that the Europeans had stolen their land and that that was why the tribe had no land for expansion, was causing deep divisions within the tribe. The tribe could no longer perform one of its major group functions. Its members scattered widely in search of employment and returned from the towns with new ideas which did not fit in with tradition. Old status relationships were breaking up. Long before the Kikuyu had tried to remedy their own affairs. They had seized on education as the cure and established the Kikuyu independent schools. These were outside, and against, the government assisted mission schools. As the position in Kikuyuland worsened, however, these became more political instruments directed against the government and the Europeans (and, incidentally, against the churches). The movement, while looking forward politically, looked backward to the roots of the tribe as well. The tribe, however, was not united and became effectively split into those who had land and those who had not or who had so little that they could not live off it. This is, of course, too simple a division. There were many cross-currents. There were many Kikuyu Christians, while the old traditions supported those who had land. The situation deteriorated to such an extent that the growing group of Kikuyu political leaders were strongly opposed to anything that the government wished to do. While, therefore, the

Kikuyu were, perhaps, the most ready for change they were intensely hostile to the government. This meant that some of the best land in Africa was barely developed and was supporting in increasing poverty a population well below what it could support if fully developed. And nothing could be done about it. This situation gave rise to the Mau Mau and erupted in the Emergency of 1952.

It is difficult to get to the bottom of this amorphous movement. It will become more difficult to do so in time as it becomes converted into the Kenya Freedom Movement, as the details are forgotten and as interest shapes history. It had its roots in the breakdown of the tribal structure under the pressures that I have described. From the pressures the new Kikuyu leaders arose, pressures which they helped to create. It was mixed up with the larger visions of their chief leader who used it but was unable to control it. Basically it was an eruption of Kikuyu 'have-nots', but many other threads ran through its complex weave; an amount of nationalism; an amount of tribal assertiveness; an amount of anti-European feeling; old traditions versus an attempt to build new traditions; Christianity versus tribal gods. The casualty figures alone demonstrate that it was, in essence, a struggle within the tribe, a spasm in a social structure. It would be fair to say that most of the participants had only vague ideas of what it was about, quite apart from the opportunists who changed sides with frequency from Mau Mau to Home Guard and back again. It was, however, action in a situation that was becoming intolerable and, in this, attracted many Kikuyu who could feel that they were doing something, no matter what, that was positive. A large part of the tribe resisted. The movement could not appeal directly to custom and tradition for support, since these would have supported the existing order. So it distorted to an incredible degree things that were customary. In this, as worse elements progressively attained influence, and the course of the movement caused this to be so, it became so obscene and disgusting that it alienated not only very many Kikuyu (and, anyway, those with land were fighting to retain what they had got) but also the rest of the world, from whence might, otherwise, have come strong movements of sympathy as well as ideological support (which are far from being the same thing).

From the economic point of view the Emergency was the best thing that could have happened to the Kikuyu. Instead of revolution from below and chaos in a situation which the revolutionaries could not themselves remedy it made possible the agrarian and land revolution that was seen to be necessary. The Mau Mau had no effect on the advance of the European economy beyond a momentary check before the momentum was restored. In Kikuyuland a new situation was created. The political opposition to the government was behind bars. It was possible to seek the co-operation of the rest, a rapidly growing number, and to get it. The government was, at least, respected, if not feared. With financial assistance from Britain the Swynnerton Plan was launched in 1954. This plan was a brilliant synthesis of the conclusions reached by research and experiment and of the various projects for development. It provided for the intensified development of African agriculture throughout the whole country and its integration in the market economy. The new economic small-holdings, which had already proved themselves in Kipsigis country, where there were no land pressures and only enclosure and the registration of freehold titles was needed, could now be applied generally, beginning with the fragmented Kikuyu lands. The plan was a revolution but on a long time-scale and it allowed itself 50 years to take place. It owed much to R. O. Hennings, then Chairman of the African Land Development Board, to L. H. Brown for his work on African farming systems and farm economics which paralleled A. Storrar's work on the European farming systems, and to G. Gamble, whose faith in the possibilities of small-holder tea planting in the face of all opinion, was to be proved triumphantly right. The government was fortunate to have in its service at that time enthusiastic official entrepreneurs of this kind. The Kenya of the future, whatever its attitude to Europeans, should inscribe these names, at least, on its roll of honour, and the Kamba particularly the name of T. Hughes-Rice who carried out the re-conditioning of the Machakos lands, turning them from a perennial famine area into a productive one.

The agricultural revolution proceeded unevenly. It went ahead more rapidly than had ever been imagined in the Kikuyu areas. The whole of Kikuyuland is now consolidated. Production is rising by about 15 per cent per annum. Even so, according to the Gatuguta Report,[1] the area is not more than 30 per cent developed. In other areas progress was slower, or did not start at all. This was so in the Abaluhya area and among the Luo of the plains beside Lake Victoria. In the case of the Luo, the technical problems were different; not simply to consolidate, register title and apply new small-holding systems but to convert the land by irrigation and drainage. These require discipline, not the freedom of the small-holding, as in irrigation schemes farmers must learn to conduct their operations at the same time as others and under direction. With both the Luo and the Abaluhya peoples we see the same basic problems as with the Kikuyu and the same reactions to them; increasing poverty, land being flooded, soil being washed away. As the people became poorer they clung closer to their traditional habits. Their political leaders supported them in opposing the government's plans. For ten years the government set aside funds for tackling these areas but failed to gain local support. They were unable to gain even the small acreage required for a pilot irrigation scheme. Nor has independence changed the attitude of the Luo, while the administrative

[1] Government Printer, Nairobi, 1963.

and technical skill for carrying out such a project is ebbing away and there is now unlikely ever to be the possibility of such a scheme.

It may, however, be doubted if the possibility was really there. The reason for opposition is more fundamental and sharper in the case of an irrigation scheme. The man is being asked to surrender his land rights in return for a tenancy in an irrigation scheme. He will not like the discipline. The scheme is a new project, and not merely the adaptation of an old way of living, and he may fail. If he fails he will lose his new rights and be unable to regain his old. Mainly, of course, it is fear of the unknown. One is forced to conclude that new irrigation schemes can only be started on unoccupied, or nearly unoccupied, land.

More recently there has been some enthusiasm among other tribes for land consolidation and enclosure. They have seen what has happened to the Kikuyu who are beginning to acquire wealth. They fear being left behind as a poor tribe. As it is better understood its advantages can be seen by those who have land rights and can secure them in perpetuity, and can borrow money on the security of their land. It does not, however, solve the problem of the landless by providing them with land. Their hope lies in employment on the developing holdings of the landed, but the fortune that has made some landed and some landless is not accepted easily by the latter.

The Swynnerton Plan implied a complete change in the basis of the economy and the disappearance of the idea that everyone must, or can, have some land. It implied a landed and landless class. In this it recognized the economic forces that were already at work, particularly among the Kikuyu. It looked farther ahead to the time when the poorer, smaller holdings would be sold and incorporated in larger farming units and a larger scale agriculture would be possible. It further implied that the landless would live (and not merely earn money) by employment. This could be done either in agriculture or in industry. If the momentum of Kenya's development were maintained all this seemed quite possible without individual hardship, and the colonial administration was already raising the minimum wage to a family wage level and beginning to plan a social security system for wage-earners to replace the social security of land. The important thing in agriculture was to ensure that every acre of land came under the control of someone who was able, and wanted, to develop it fully, to extract the maximum production from it. By creating individual land ownership the plan produced a situation in which it was expected that this would happen naturally in the course of time, as those who were not 'real farmers' sold their land to those who were. Every man in Kenya wants to own land but not every man wants to be a farmer. As the land came into the hands of the more enterprising so development would increase. As development increased so would employment on the land. There is, of course, a limit to this, when the farm is large enough to replace men with machines. Generally, however, the function of the machine is to cope with a labour shortage, either general or in those peak periods in the farming year when the farm labour force is too small to cope. (These, in turn, produce peak periods at which all machinery is in demand. Interesting cost studies can be made, on a national and farm basis, to indicate the relatively low cost of extra labour.)

There were dangers in the plan. The idea of a landless class would not readily be accepted, even though the reality was already in being. The rigidity introduced into the actuality of landed and landless by the registration of titles would cause tensions. The success of the plan depended on continued, rapid, economic advance in the country in both agriculture and industry, so that the landless could be mopped up in other employment while the government was laying its plans for a new social security system. Firm administration and the maintenance of order were essential during the transition period while the new situation was gaining acceptance. (Compare what was said earlier about the use of physical force in preventing (undesirable) change while a new situation establishes itself in which the need for force for that end becomes unnecessary. If order could be maintained during this period then the new situation would become the accepted mode of things and force would no longer be necessary. The country would have been set on a new course. When a sailing ship changes course there is a period when absolute discipline is required. When the new course is set, and everything has settled in its proper place, the captain and crew can relax.) Any severe setback to the economy would aggravate the tensions and cause great instability. Virtually the plan required a continuance of colonial administration if its fruits were to be garnered.

African employment of labour tends to be at a lower cost than European. Wages are lower. The trade union approach is to the better organized European employers. The African employers are not organized, are too widely scattered, and can ignore the unions in view of the many unemployed. They tend, however, to follow the European pattern of employment on farms, through the Resident Labourer with his own small food plot. The cost of this on a small farm with good land in reducing the area that can be brought under maximum production for the market has yet to become a serious factor.

We have already noted how employment on the land is related to the development of the land and the capital put into it. Most developed European farms employ a large quantity of labour. Nothing is gained and a lot lost, in managerial skill and 'know-how', in dispossessing Europeans of fully-developed farms. The same can be said of semi-developed farms unless the new owners have access to more capital and have equivalent skills and know-how. There was every reason to believe that the Swynnerton Plan would, in the African areas, automatically select the best African farm entrepreneurs, put the land in their possession and attain maximum production. It would then attain maximum employment on the land. Even the areas that now appear overcrowded could support a larger population than exists. But it all takes time and requires the maintenance, if necessary by force, of stability. In a sense, of course, it only postpones the evil day as the population continues to increase, but it so expands the economy and spreads wealth widely through the people that new markets are created for industry which, with the general growth in production and services, would bid fair to mop up the expanding population.

In considering the philosophy of the Swynnerton Plan it is worth commenting on the rôle of the entrepreneur or capitalist of whatever size and at whatever level in a developing community. Many have pointed out the lack of this person as the great handicap in under-developed countries. Because he makes money he is subject to criticism and the new African rich are already being attacked by their fellows. 'Is this African Socialism?' we are asked. We noted earlier the successful railway promoter of the last century, not in any criticism but to demonstrate his identity of interest with the developments of his time. We have noted the need to bring every acre of land into the hands of those who will make the best use of it. This means the men whose self-interest is identical with that purpose. If this is not done, progress and development will be slower. The Swynnerton Plan set out to bring together the interests of the country and the self-interest of the individual. This seems wholly desirable and one of the functions of government, as it is to curb the individual when his self-interest conflicts with

E

the national interest. By harnessing self-interest to public ends the economy gains its greatest motor force. The important thing is not to allow the capitalist to control the government. The need to control the self-interest of the individual is often confused with the idea that the government must do everything. This is a misunderstanding of the art of government.

The other side of the Swynnerton Plan coin, however good it might be from an economic point of view, was its effect on the social structure. The principle of individual land-ownership, brought into being at a given point in time (although that point varied from district to district), cut across tribal traditions. The tribe could no longer pretend to shoulder its responsibilities for finding land for its members. That it had not been able to do so for some time in the overcrowded areas had not removed the principle. Nor did the plan do so immediately. The introduction of the new class structure did not reflect traditional class structures and traditions. Africans, particularly the early-affected Kikuyu, found themselves more sharply divided and bewildered. Not only were there landed and landless. The former included the progressive farmer who had fully adopted the new ways and was rapidly making himself part of the money economy and becoming 'rich'. It also included those who were still thinking in terms of traditional agriculture although anxious to secure their own land titles. The landless were driven back on to traditional ways that gave them no comfort, and they had found, in the Mau Mau, that tradition did not support them. Having failed to secure their end in the distortion of tradition they began to look to independence to solve their problems and to an African government under which they would find new land for subsistence agriculture on the European farms. They transferred the land-finding function of the tribe to an independent African government.

The general background of the country and its inheritance at *uhuru* is beginning to take shape. In this pattern are the economic problems that an independent government must face and tackle.

Negligible mineral resources preclude a break out into heavy industry. Development must continue to be in agriculture, with industry supplying the new markets that agricultural development creates. As industry grows and efficiency improves there are export markets for it and for agricultural produce in the Indian Ocean area, in spite of transport difficulties and the distance of the heart of Kenya from the sea. The impact of a money economy on a society whose thinking was in stereotyped traditional forms was causing disequilibria and instabilities and giving rise to a new kind of political leader; still a tribal leader but different from the traditional authorities.

Development was progressing rapidly, if unevenly, in both the European and African sectors. Capital flowed in easily. There was an efficient administration, first-class technical services, a highly organized developmental structure and a supply of entrepreneurs and skills which was rare in under-developed countries.

Against this was a growing population and increasing landlessness in the old overcrowded areas where tribal instability was greatest.

The government was coping with the revolutionary effects of the money economy. It knew what to do and its plans were sound. It needed, however, another ten to twenty years of firm government before it could establish Kenya as one of the developed and prosperous countries of Africa. Although there were many forces working against it, they did not appear to be uncontrollable. The growing instabilities seemed unlikely to topple over before the new course had been set.

This was a limited view which ignored a number of other

factors of greater importance. In theory, however, an independent government can pick up the threads and continue the progress, having, perhaps, by its coming into being resolved the other difficulties. Does *uhuru* signify things that prevent this happening?

Before answering this question we must look at the other factors that determine the shape of *uhuru*, its direction and speed.

CHAPTER THREE

The Immigrant Races

THE attitudes of the immigrant races have a considerable, if not decisive, bearing on the form that *uhuru* takes. In Kenya the matter is complicated by having two immigrant races, European and Asian, whose attitudes differed and who did not merge among themselves. We have noted that the imperial Indian government sought the same privileges in land for Asians as Europeans. In commerce and industry there seemed no difference between the position of the European and Asian. Because, however, of their different attitudes I shall consider them separately, if only to underline the similarity of their positions.

THE EUROPEANS

To understand something of the attitudes of the Europeans one must know something of the society from which they came. Being British one would expect their effect on Kenya to differ from that of French, Portuguese and Belgians on their colonies. Any analysis of *uhuru* in British colonies will not, therefore, be valid for other countries, although the dominating influences may be the same. The emergent pattern will be different to the extent that the outlooks of the settlers' home countries differ. This is seen to be the case. It is possible to group together all sorts of colonial rule because all will have a large number of common features, and to be against them all (or even, conceivably, for them all—perish the thought!) and yet to distinguish between different kinds.

Colonial rule is an expression covering forms rather than reality. It exists within countries whose boundaries no one would dream of questioning, wherein there is a recognizable minority group which is not fully integrated, or able to integrate, with the majority, and which occupies a clearly defined homeland; Kurds in Iraq, Nagas and Goans in India, Esthonians in the Soviet Union. South Africa is engaged in creating colonies within its borders. It can vary in degree. It exists in the 'satellite' form in Eastern Europe and in the 'banana' republics of Central America. In these cases an alien minority or government decides a greater or lesser number of issues in a country which is otherwise recognized as being 'independent'. The Hungarian uprising demonstrated the limitations to its independence. Cuba, presumably, simply changed its overlord or protector. Even the legal integration of Algeria with France did not prevent their separation. 'Colonialism' is, therefore, little more than an overt recognition of an existing state of affairs, and the term applies only to its manifestation between white and coloured races. The fundamental dependence of the minor party is voiced in cries of 'neo-colonialism' when 'independence' is achieved. This expresses the exasperation of finding that there is no such thing as national freedom, only degrees of freedom, depending on a country's internal economic strength. A country can achieve a measure of real freedom if it is willing to abandon the pursuit of wealth and retire into isolation like the hermits in the Egyptian desert in the early centuries of our era, or like the tribes of Africa before the coming of the European. Europe was parcelled out after the first world war on the principle of self-determination based on linguistic affinities, modified in part by the need to create viable units. (Who now recalls the arguments about Macedonian independence?) Africa has been parcelled out on the basis of quite arbitrary colonial boundaries which have no logical self-deterministic significance but represent a stage in the growth of nation-building achieved under colonial rule. This nation-building was often more apparent than real. The alternative was a host of petty tribal states and a return to the Africa that existed before. The fact that this division has been accepted by African leaders implies that colonial rule was at least a politically constructive thing. Yet the new African leaders in different countries have much in common with each other, so that there appears to be almost an African nationality. Attempts to create larger units, however, either by the colonial powers or by Africans, have failed in ignoring the geography of Africa.[1]

Having said, then, that colonial rule is merely a particular form of something that appears all over the world, this particular form has a number of common features and some differences depending on the colonial power.

The British who came to Africa came from a highly stratified and class-conscious society, although there was opportunity for mobility between classes, unlike the situation in India, and unlike that which was to emerge in Africa. 'Gentlemen' could be distinguished from 'players' not only by accent and dress, but in a hundred other ways to the practised observer. All were practised observers and knew how to 'place' themselves in relation to others. The lower classes were not understood. There was thought to be nothing to understand, only something to control. This was the pattern chiefly of the countryside, particularly in the south of England, and it was largely from the countryside that the early immigrants came. They came to a situation that they could recognize and one with the added advantage that you could tell immediately by his skin colour to which class a man belonged.

There had been difficulties in West Africa where it had been necessary to import a number of tradesmen and fore-

[1] And, of course, politics. Leaders whose position depends on a national political base are reluctant to venture their fortune in a wider field and, indeed, they represent national interests that will conflict at many obvious points with those of their neighbours.

men from the lower middle classes in Britain, in the absence
of Asians to play this rôle. This was arranged for in Accra
by having two European clubs; one for first-class officials
and one for second-class officials. This survived until the
early 1930s when the economies caused by the depression
so depleted the ranks of the second-class officials that their
club disappeared. Africans, too, were very conscious of this
British class division. Servants who had worked for a first-
class official would not lower their own status by working
for a second-class official. (In this they were no different
from servants in England.) The press, when it attacked
Europeans, was usually careful to single out second-class
officials. West Africans at that time fully accepted the
'gentlemen' and 'players' approach and the gentleman myth
that went with it. This was that the gentleman is well-
behaved and a man of honour. On the side of the gentleman
himself it is that his privileged position gives him particular
responsibilities, particularly the obligation to behave honour-
ably, and that by doing so he is entitled to his privileged
position. This was accepted on both sides, and British rule
rested to a degree on this convention of superiority of behaviour. Considerable pains were taken to ensure that it was
lived up to, both in selection for the civil service from the
class that was thought likely to provide men of honour and
by the quick removal of those who clearly betrayed the
idea. The large numbers of Europeans of all kinds to appear
in West Africa during the war made it impossible to maintain this position. The sand castle crumbled away in the tide.
In addition, West Africans had long demonstrated their
ability to run affairs and were the executive arm in most
government offices. Nothing remained between them and
full authority except the gentleman-superiority myth. Even
the fact that many Europeans did not, in fact, behave like
superior gentlemen did not, before the war, dim the myth.
When faced with reality the African pushed the myth back

in time. It was possible to read in the African press references to 'the old-time honesty of the Englishman' when disapproving or approving of some particular action.[1]

In Kenya the situation was both easier and more complex in that the second-class position was largely held by Asians. All Europeans had to be absorbed into one class. This was not really done and Europeans had to weigh each other up as in England. The classless white society was never achieved in the way it was in South Africa. With the new post-war flood of immigrants the superiority myth became untenable.

[1] It is interesting to note, however, that this general acceptance of racial differences was not accompanied by positive segregational measures, although by 1938 these measures, which were to intensify throughout Africa after the war, made a small appearance when a new Colonial Secretary in Accra started a church for Europeans only. This caused the greatest resentment among those Europeans who had been accustomed to attending the African services and who continued to do so.

The segregationist feeling can, perhaps, be attributed to the appearance of great numbers of European women in West Africa. Sir Michael Blundell once put forward the theory that three things caused segregation; the lavatory, the bath and the white woman. Before they arrived the European man performed under the tree like everyone else, did not bath and smelt like everyone else and gained a good local knowledge at night. With the arrival of the lavatory he performed in private and began to think of himself as something different. This was confirmed by the arrival of the bath, when he realized that he smelt different. Finally, the arrival of the European woman cut him off from his nightly association with the local news sources.

Seriously, however, there seems to have been a growth of a segregationist feeling in Britain, stemming perhaps, however indirectly, from Nazism and Fascism, which by the end of the war had produced a situation in which a very large proportion of British emigrants to the colonies went with a sense that they were entering a superior class and a determination not to mix with the natives. This was particularly apparent among those whose own social standing in Britain was dubious, the 'temporary gentlemen' of the wartime army officers. (A small group of such were able to change the non-racial Belize Club in British Honduras into a whites-only club.)

Many of the new immigrants clearly lacked the gentleman's principles but were quick to grasp his privileges. This was what they had understood of the Kenya that they had seen during the war. Africans entered a new world in which they might even find themselves cheated by a European. Even the gentleman himself became somewhat tarnished, as no conventions of society compelled him to maintain standards and the group had become too large for internal discipline. The approach became more like this: because I am a gentleman and therefore honourable, everything that I do, no matter how crooked, is in fact honourable.

This digression on gentleman-superiority is not without significance. When the principle existed it was accepted on both sides as the justification for ruling and being ruled. When it disappeared the justification had gone. Partly it derived from the self-conscious superiority of the first-comers and, perhaps, they were, indeed, largely gentlemen. After the war no one, even in England, believed any longer in the idea of the gentleman, and the self-confidence in the colonial position was ebbing. 'Colonialism', in losing its nobility, became simply a matter of being in the thing for its advantages. This attitude became more dominant as the emphasis was put on economic development in the post-war period. One was a member less of an élite than of a ruling class, albeit an efficient, intelligent and enterprising one.

There was thus transferred to Kenya with ease the British class structure and it continued into the new post-war era. Fortunately the Asians knew their place. It was a familiar one in their home country. They did not threaten the structure even when a few of their number attained wealth and eminence and more or less joined the ruling class. (It is an interesting commentary on men's real scales of value that as many Asians as could get in continued to come to East Africa even though it lay under the rule of the hated coloni-

alist, in preference to the poverty of independent India.)
The Africans were clearly the lowest class. Attitudes were
reinforced by the immigration of Europeans from India
who sought to enjoy in Kenya their previous privileged
position. The position became more difficult to maintain
as the post-war immigration from Britain was clearly not a
descent of gods, but of people who nevertheless expected to
be treated like gods. The Roman Empire, with no real
colour problems, appears in retrospect to have been free
from this particular class and race difficulty and to have
successfully absorbed its subject peoples so that they became
an integral part of the structure and could adopt it as their
own. The seizure of power by the imperial army from the
republican senate increasingly opened the empire to all its
peoples, and vertical mobility became possible. This was
not possible in Kenya because entry into the ruling class was
closed and attitudes insisted on keeping it closed. This is why
a change in power means an elimination of the previous
rulers rather than the non-racial mutual absorption that was
thought possible for a time.

The matter can be looked at in another way. The European immigrants were, in a broad sense, functional. They
came from Britain as administrators, farmers, executives or
entrepreneurs. The numbers incapable of performing their
function were small. Similarly the Asian immigration was
functional (and necessary): the craftsmen, shopkeepers,
clerks and junior executives. The Africans, although originally all subsistence agriculturalists or pastoralists, were a
complete people and not a section of a people. No doubt
they had their mute, inglorious Miltons and their village
Hampdens. Once they began to move out of subsistence
production and acquired education, once they began to
learn about the new way of living in the world, they began
to separate themselves into the able, medium able and less
able. This might often be the more or less adaptable. The

educational system might not be complete but it began to
sift people. No matter how able, however, they were confined to an inferior status with practically no opportunity
of breaking through. Even when they did the same job they
were paid less for it, on the ground that they needed a lower
standard of living, or were used to one. This made mixing
impossible. There may have been stronger forces than that
at work to prevent mixing, but no one can mix easily with
others at a different income level and standard of living.
Patronage is inescapable on the one side and occurs among
those Europeans who make it a principle to mix. Well-
meaning attempts to select the more brilliant Africans for
training abroad to fill some humble post on their return
only accentuated the problem.

(It is interesting to note that the Africans after independence have justified a very rapid rate of 'Africanization' of
the civil service on the ground that the service should reflect
the numerical proportions of the different races in the
country. There may be grounds of political expediency for
doing so, but the argument is nonsense and ignores the very
special and functional nature of the immigrant races that we
have noted.)

One of the arguments supporting differential rates of pay
was related to the supposition that every African employee
had some land in the African Reserves. This might well have
been true, but it meant that the employee *had* to have some
land. This ensured that he kept a foot in both worlds. In the
lower rungs of the civil service it often meant that clerks
came into a busy, modern office by day and returned in the
evening to a hut in the Reserve. They put one foot in the
new world but kept one in the old. It is not surprising that
they adapted uneasily to the new world and seemed, on
their daily emergence into it from a world of different ways,
habits and attitudes, relatively inefficient in it. This effect of
the way the class structure was applied presented the African

with immense psychological difficulties. However adaptable, he was prevented from making a full adaptation.

We have noted earlier how the economy of Kenya was for a long time the European sector. This arose from natural causes and we have also seen the difficulties in getting the African sector moving. The European paid most of the taxes and expected them to be spent in his own interest. He had overcome some of the natural handicaps of living at a great distance from the sea by concentrating on quality products for export. He feared possible world overproduction in the various commodities that he produced. He knew that the small marginal producer of high quality goods could always find a good market. He, therefore, feared that African development in the same products would swamp him with lower quality goods bearing the Kenya label. In the end the Swynnerton Plan had to be financed from foreign aid, although the European presence, and all that went with it, enabled foreign aid to be more easily procured and a more effective start to be made.

The European farmer had also gained control of the economy. We have noted the wide array of statutory marketing organizations. The government was only able to gain consent to their establishment, after hard argument, by conceding effective control to the producers—in fact, the European producers. Each board was usually controlled ultimately by a producer board elected by the European farmers. The Agriculture Act of 1955 enshrined the division of the economy into two parts in the law. It set up two Boards of Agriculture; the one based on a pyramid of local elected area committees and sub-committees in the scheduled areas; the other based on a pyramid of district committees, part nominated, part elected, in the African (or non-scheduled) areas. The latter was a serious attempt to move in the African areas to a system more akin to that in the European areas at a time when there was, at last, a prospect of developing African agriculture. The African board apportioned funds made available on a widespread array of small development projects and brought in local consultation. It attempted to associate the African farmer with his own development problems. The European board, however, represented the virtual handing over of the European economy to the European farmer. There was always a European farmer as Minister for Agriculture. Without this the relations of the settlers with the government would have been intolerable. The European settlers already controlled the marketing organizations, although ultimate power was reserved to the Minister, and protected themselves by production controls and licensing. The system was, nevertheless, a reasonable attempt, at that stage in the country's growth, to set up organizations adapted to the needs of the two sectors.

Its disadvantage was that it encouraged the European farmer to be inward-looking and to think in a world in which African problems, except that of labour, did not exist for him. African problems were for the government not for the settler. He had effective power but not responsibility. The quite genuine fear of quality deterioration concealed a more real fear that, if Africans produced the same goods as Europeans, they would bring down the price and put the Europeans out of business. All African development was, therefore, an object of suspicion, including the Swynnerton Plan. Between 1954, when the plan began, and 1960, a series of questions was asked in the predominantly European legislative council about how much of the government's money was going on African and how much on European agriculture, designed to find out if Africans were getting more than their fair share in relation to the share that they paid of taxes. The 'best' question was asked after the government had done some modest propaganda on the fact that it was giving credit to African farmers and encouraging them to take credit. There was a predictable reaction of alarm. 'How much credit had been given respectively to European and to African farmers in the year?' The answer was about £3 million to Europeans (including short-term credit) and under £150,000 to Africans. The Minister arranged for the question to be withdrawn.[1]

This inward-looking attitude was exemplified as late as 1961, at a time when the Europeans had still not grasped the significance of *uhuru* and their ebbing power. Farmers received a rebate of the tax levied on diesel oil. It was used in tractors, and the tax would otherwise have been an addition to agricultural production costs. The refund was, in fact, enjoyed almost entirely by Europeans, although it was sound enough whoever enjoyed it. The Minister felt that it would be vulnerable after *uhuru* and proposed to replace it by a fertilizer subsidy. This would have agricultural benefits and be shared by Africans. This meant that, since the size of the subsidy was limited to the size of the rebate, Europeans would receive less because of the African participation. On the other hand, a fertilizer subsidy would clearly arouse no opposition and the Europeans would get something instead of the nothing that was likely under an African government. A reasonable enough proposition, one would think, even if it over-estimated, perhaps, the degree of attention to detail that an African government was likely to give. The proposal was, therefore, put to the European board of agriculture. After the explanation of the reasons each member (each a chairman of a local agricultural committee) was asked for his opinion. Each in turn said: 'No. This is our money. We pay the taxes. Why should we share it with Africans?' (Not an exact quotation.) In all of this, of

[1] The low figure for African loans was due, at the start, to the difficulties noted earlier of giving credit to African farmers; as these difficulties were overcome the disparity was reduced.

course, the European farmer was doing no more than his counterpart in Britain. He had built up a structure modelled on that of Britain, and he struggled and fought, as did his British counterpart, for every penny that he could extract from the rest of the community. In his case, the rest of the community included the African farmer. This narrow concentration would have mattered less if the African had been as well organized and equipped to fight on the same terms. He was not. The African representatives on their board knew much too little of how the economy really worked or of how to argue and get their ends—indeed, of what ends should they be trying to get. They were up against a much more educated and knowledgeable opposition. Their inferior position, as Africans, made them weak. In their areas power passed to a new generation of politicians. As one African leader of the late 1940s and early 1950s, now long since by-passed, said, 'If we advocate to our people co-operation with the Europeans and always come back empty-handed from talks with them how can we keep their support and pursue reasonable courses?'

The European settler made an enormous contribution to Kenya and brought inestimable benefits to the country. (An Ethiopian recently joked, 'If they don't want the white settlers in Kenya, send them up here. We need them.') But they were showing signs of being a check on African development at a time when Africans were ready to advance. How had the Europeans attained to this position of power?

Southern Rhodesia obtained internal self-government in 1923 and showed no wish for more. Independence involved considerable expense for no real return. There was nothing to fear. Defence could be left to Britain. It seemed improbable that British foreign policy could be different from Rhodesia's. Rhodesia, without a thought, made a full contribution in the second world war. Europeans in Kenya sought the same position but without success. They were too few. It was not that there were any doubts about the continuation of European settlement or of an enclave in East Africa pursuing a European way of life. Nor were they a 'protectorate' as was Northern Rhodesia. Their failure to gain the government had the effect of making the 'Government' the enemy. In Southern Rhodesia, after internal self-government, the civil service became local and worked very closely with the settlers in partnership. In Kenya the 'Government' of officials, ostensibly answering to an authority in Britain, became the enemy. This was symbolized in the big sporting event of the year, the Officials *v.* Settlers cricket match, a dour struggle but played within the rules.

The settlers battled at every point with the official government and usually did so successfully, so that in the final outcome their power was little less than that of the Rhodesian settlers. As economic man incarnate they pushed, pulled and squeezed the government at every turn and, incidentally, produced as a result a highly efficient civil service. We have seen how they obtained control of the agricultural economy. Every move that the officials thought of taking they scrutinized carefully to assess the settlers' reaction. Then they submitted it to one of the many boards that the settler had been able to insist on, with powers to advise the government and the right to be asked for advice. In few countries are government policies subject to such close, detailed and grinding examination. They were often improved as a result, but they always took account of the settlers' wishes. There was another reason for this tenderness. The settlers had powerful connections in England and were able to bring some weight to bear on the British government through these connections. They were aided in this by the method of selection of the top echelon of the civil service, the administration. These men were chosen as likely to have a similar outlook and background to the influential settler.

F

In theory it should have strengthened the government *vis à vis* the settler. In practice it made the administrator vulnerable to the accusation of letting his own side down. Basically, he identified himself with the settler and carefully distinguished himself from other civil servants. The settlers responded, even when violently attacking the civil service and the government, by praising the administration. The influence of the settlers in Britain could too, conceivably, influence the civil servant's career in the higher reaches.

The settlers, therefore, kept up a barrage of propaganda and were able to gain control of the all-important Ministry of Agriculture when the ministerial system of government began at the end of the 'forties. They were able to entrench themselves firmly in control of every statutory organization. A colonial administration is very sensitive to pressures, particularly in detail, and tries to resolve or dissolve them when they arise. African pressures were, however, weakly felt because they were badly expressed, and there was a less sharp sensitivity towards them. The early African leaders went away empty-handed because, although they were expressing real discontents, their general knowledge of the situation was insufficient for them to express their points effectively. Instead of searching for the real difficulty that they were trying to express, it was often easy to show that the particular point that they made was wrong. To dig below this to the real discontent, the spring of their trouble, demanded more patience and time than people wished to give. It was inevitable that the African leadership should pass from these men to others who would simply take the attitude that until the colonial administration was got rid of there would be no chance of Africans getting a proper hearing or of their problems being dealt with. This was rather unfair on the colonial administration, which always considered carefully all complaints. Its blind spot was that it did not realize that African complaints were symptoms of disease rather than the disease itself. European and Asian complaints were different. (This, again, is not a problem that is eliminated by independence. An independent African government has the same problem in the exertion of pressures and in understanding what the real complaint is. Its weakness is that it tends to take the stated complaint at its face value and to make adjustments to meet it which do nothing to solve the real problem underneath and may even exacerbate it. Fundamentally this is a problem of communication in a country largely illiterate, where the people's horizons are limited by their immediate environment.)

It may be worth examining the methods the Europeans used to apply pressure. The only period when the government exercised real control had been during the war, and in the hangover period after it, when it was recognized that greater issues were at stake and when the settler had to accept that there were fields of necessity in which he could not be the judge because of ignorance of the total situation. (At that time he was more in the position of the African leaders.) In that period the government had been able to hold producer prices down in the basic foodstuffs; wheat and maize. The government made profits from grain trading which it used to erect a grain storage network over the country. This stood it in good stead later on and it was able to rationalize grain transport and effect great savings in the cost of movement of wheat and maize. This was used by the European farmers' representatives to attack the government, on the ground that it had deprived them of six (or was it nine?) million pounds of income. This charge was made regularly at the annual price review and was an admirable starting point for claiming increased prices. The civil servants hung their heads in shame at the dreadful deed that they had done and were suitably contrite and sympathetic in the ensuing negotiations. Prices were based on costs of production; a simple enough notion but one which no economist has successfully defined in mixed farming without leaving ample room for argument.

The grain storage provided from the early profits of the government was used by the European farmer as a means of increasing the strategic reserve. Who knew what war might not be around the corner and had not Kenya had to grow and hold supplies for all East Africa in the last war? So each year a little was added to the strategic reserve. This enabled the export of surpluses at the lower post-war prices to be avoided and a higher pay-out to be made to the farmer. This only came to an end when the Mau Mau Emergency used up the government's financial reserves and it was no longer able to finance this growing stockpile. This example shows how the continued pressure was maintained, particularly at any point that affected the European settler's pocket. The administration were unable to combat him in actual debate. This would have demanded a knowledge of economic and financial matters that did not come from being a district commissioner in the Beau Geste country of the Northern Frontier one day and an under-secretary in a ministry the next. When the government engaged an agricultural economist for an eighteen-month study of wheat and maize production costs and he produced better evidence than the farmers, the latter abandoned production costs as a basis for fixing prices and resorted to more general pressures.

An example of this may be seen with crop advances. These were made to farmers from government funds through the Kenya Farmers' Association (Co-op) Ltd; a large organization handling a lot of farmers' produce and supplying them with equipment, etc., on credit. The actual authority for issuing advances was delegated to the Association and its staff. The Association in turn issued its own credit in the knowledge that it could back the credit by issuing government crop advances later. If they were not recovered that was unfortunate. (This is, of course, an over-simplification of the complete entanglement of the two sources of credit.) The bill for outstanding government advances was beginning to look uncomfortably large. The government had legal provisions to protect its interest but these had not been applied. The Ministry finally decided to disentangle its own credit from the Association's and to apply the provisions of the law. At that point the President of the Association and some of his committee descended upon the Minister for Finance, said that the Association was in difficult financial circumstances, that the Ministry's action would ruin it and that the farmers would be ruined at the same time. The officials were told to keep their hands off the Association. Three months later the Association accounts showed a stronger position than ever and an increased dividend for members. The lesson was learnt by the Association but not by ministers. After that, every year at the date when the ministry officials had time to start up that particular hare again, a rumour would go round that the Association was going bankrupt. A note from the Minister would be passed down, saying: 'Hands off the Association: they are in financial trouble.' The fact that this would be denied by the Association's financial controller over the telephone was not allowed to have any influence. Too many persons had been involved and committed themselves for the complicated facts to have any bearing. Three months later the Association would declare higher dividends again.

In extreme cases marches of Europeans on Parliament Buildings or Government House were organized. But these were often only the expression of frayed nerves and tempers at the end of the dry season.

We have noted, then, three forms of pressure: (i) in negotiation by the representatives of an extremely intelligent minority group; this was limited to details, usually with a marked financial implication, on a subject on which they were well-informed; it did not apply to the non-agricultural and non-financial aspects of government policy; (ii) pressure on politicians; (iii) wider pressures to frighten the government on to, or off, some course.

The second of these prompts a closer look at the actual working of politics. These are not peculiar to Kenya or to the European politician, although what one might term the second generation African politician did not participate until after independence. Prior to independence his whole effort was directed to its achievement and the normal political game was in abeyance. The first generation African politician had tried it but had failed to compete with Europeans.

It must not be concluded from the Crop Advances Case that ministers, even civil service ministers, ignore facts or are easily misled. It is most unusual for them to be misled. Each minister is supplied by the civil service and by pressure groups with various facts, complaints, issues, etc., which form the counters with which they play the game. Other politicians are in the same position, except that they do not get supplied with the official counters. Civil service ministers have their career at stake as well. They may be bidding for the Governorship of Wagawaga. The politician will be playing for maximum support either for some policy dear to his heart or for himself. The two may be the same, since, if he does not play for himself, he will not achieve his policy. His policy may, at the highest level, be some general aim, such as the advancement of his country or, at a lower level, of his tribe, race, group, etc. The more general his aim the more opportunist he will often appear. The counters that the politicians are supplied with are then used for exchange. This one is dropped in return for support on that one, with the object of achieving some general or specific end. Those whose ends are more general survive longest in the game since they have more flexibility in play. Where there is an electoral system they have to declare some of their counters and cannot then easily exchange these. Public speeches are such declarations of their hands, but cover only a limited part. The counters all have different values and part of the politician's success lies in judging accurately the value, and in discarding a low value one in exchange for a high value one. If he misjudges and discards a high value one, he may find that someone else has picked it up. So others' causes are exchanged until the player has furthered his own cause. This is why matters of facts and figures tend to be merely playthings unless they further some politician's main cause. In the case of the Crop Advances the facts and figures were a very low value counter, compared with the gain from an impression of sweet reasonableness and from a declaration of a determination to support the Association. It would only become significant if the facts and figures came before Parliament through the Public Accounts Committee, and that was a politically conscious body to which officials answered, not ministers. In this period counters supplied by the civil service rated a low value. African politicians found their counters virtually unplayable and they only gained value if they could create disturbances about them.

The importance of the political game (and we shall have occasion later to look at it played on a much larger scale) is that it resolves, or should resolve, all the political and other pressures at work in the country, and perform like some stock or produce exchange. If the politicians assess their counters properly they should achieve the greatest degree of stability possible. A lot of counters (peoples' hopes, complaints, discontents) would have been discarded, but they should only be ones of minor value, minor causes of instability. Unfortunately the African voice was at first unheard, except through the administrative machine, whose concern was ruling rather than politics, sensitive machine as it was. Successive constitutions adjusted the balance of sound so that the African voice was more and more heard, and so that the African politician should not have to give his counters value through violence. Once he had done so they ceased to be interchangeable, and so appeared only redeemable by independence, although they were generally no more redeemable by an African government than by a colonial one.

A further weakness of the political game is that it is being played now, and very few politicians do or can play for the distant future. It is only too easy to forget that every deal they make settles some part of the pattern of the future as well. And who can see the future whole?

By using the term 'political game' I intend no criticism of politicians. I seek merely to describe how they function and what the importance of their function is, as in their dealings the country adjusts itself and seeks new equilibria. The more stable the country the more skilled they have been. It remains that they deal with things on a different plane and in a different way from both the planner and the ordinary man, and they take, of necessity, the short view. This is one of the theoretical advantages of the one-party state; it can take a long view and really consider the needs of the people. We shall see whether it is really likely to do so but we can now see one of its weaknesses. It runs the risk of great temporary instability which requires physical force to control. If, however, the position is almost totally unstable anyway, it is justified, as it was by Henry Tudor, Cromwell, Napoleon and Lenin.

We have noted, then, how the pressure that the European settler was able to bring to bear on the British government, and, through it, on the Colonial Office and the Kenya government, made him the effective ruler of Kenya within a narrow field. It did not give him responsibility for Kenya and he was insensitive to African pressure and the growing disequilibria. On the machinery of government his influence was beneficial. It was well-known that Kenya was able to do things differently from other colonies. Many things were done better. Red tape was broken with facility and the constant pressure *in detail*, which was absent from other colonies, made for a much more efficient civil service. Every action was scrutinized through a microscope albeit a distorted one. Farmers seem to have more time for this than others. It would be nice to think that, if African criticism had had a voice at the centre and had been equally detailed, it would have had a pronounced effect. This, however, is doubtful, and they could not be heard unless their instability toppled over into violence. Apart from the Kikuyu situation the disequilibria were far from that point. The administrative machine was a sensitive one and busied itself in the remedying of local minor disequilibria, but could not cope with major ones, which continued to grow. Nor would the problems which gave rise to them have been easy to explain if Europeans had had to do so. Africans were baffled. The government was well-intentioned but communicated more easily with Europeans and was emotionally geared in with them. Africans took refuge in hopes of independence when they would be arguing with their own people in terms that both understood.

It is interesting to speculate on whether things would have been different if the European settler had been responsible for Kenya, black and white, instead of ruling it through an agent. This was a system under which he could pursue his own immediate ends without having to take account of the whole country. It seems improbable. The so-called 'moderate' elements, those most alive to the country's real problems, had only a limited influence. The reason lies in the basic attitudes that I have described and which were to be expected from the history of Kenya and of its immigrants. We are beset by a feeling of inevitability; inevitable because the majority of European settlers appreciated that the proposals of the 'moderates' meant a marked change in the way of life that had been established and which had been the cause of their immigration. The 'moderates' needed a strong African voice if they were to have success. That is why they were strongest during the Mau Mau Emergency. When that had been brought under control their influence weakened and there was a wish to re-establish the old position. At the same time the Emergency destroyed the hope of the 'moderates' finding strongly voiced political allies in the largest tribe and the one with the greatest disequilibrium.

The civil service reflected the social structure of the country in its three racial tiers with different rates of pay for each race, even if doing the same job. It also showed the same obstacles to African advancement. The one exception to the general approach of Europeans was the European Civil Servants' Association. Partly because they were outside the political hurly-burly and partly because their daily contacts with the Asian and African associations enabled them to sense and feel the underlying trends more clearly, they were able to take a longer view. They were able to explain and gain support for their view from the Asians and Africans (and were probably the only European body that met the other races on an equal footing) but failed completely to explain them to the government. They had eventually to retire baffled, together with the other associations, in the face of incomprehension arising from stereotyped European attitudes. It is worth digressing to look at this little-known episode in Kenya's history because it illustrates the difficulty of achieving change without independence. In it reasonable Europeans found the same difficulty as reasonable Africans in getting action.

The story begins in 1949–50. At that time, the thought of serious change was far from every European's mind. Independence might come some day, but not in my lifetime, or that of my children or grandchildren. It was not necessary now to think of what form it would take, or what the country would be like, in that distant future. The European Civil Servants' Association, with their close consultations with the African Civil Service Association, were more conscious of the stirrings within the country than most Europeans, whose contact with educated Africans was slight; even they, however, were unaware of the imminence of the Mau Mau. At that time the trade unions were still embryonic and the African Civil Service Association contained a preponderance of the educated Africans, what I have termed the 'first generation' African leaders. It was impossible to be in daily contact with them without sensing the deep frustrations which could only lead to an outburst sooner or later. It seemed more likely to be sooner. If the existing set-up were to be maintained it could only be by suppression and a police state. At that time it seemed quite possible to control the situation by force indefinitely. Such a prospect was not a cheerful one. It could only lead to greater racial tension, to fear and to the European community becoming an alien and hated minority. It seemed to the European association that one need not be particularly clairvoyant to foresee such a situation developing and that it was necessary to take positive steps to dissolve the growing antagonisms and to try to produce a country which would be tolerable for all races, instead of one that would become intolerable for all. A civil servants' association can only operate in a limited field, but it seemed that action in the civil service could initiate change and set an example to the country, since the government was the biggest employer.

Under the leadership of Lt.-Com. J. Miller, G.C., the European association worked out with the other races a scheme for the unification of the civil service, only to be told by the Governor at that time (1950) that such a proposal was premature. This, less than two years before the Mau Mau Emergency, was a shock to the association, coming as it did from a quarter in which they had expected some sympathy. Surely the government, with all its ears to the ground, must be aware of what was happening and wish to resolve tensions?[1] Beside which, it represented a Labour government in Britain. The association was unconvinced and continued the struggle for the next three years.

They were anxious to do two things especially. The first was to ensure that Africans would have the possibility of advancement to the top, no matter at what level they entered and that the class structure of the service should be removed. Very few Africans entered above the lower levels and the classification system made it impossible for them to reach higher levels. The circumstances of Africans were such that their schooling was erratic. Parents might be unable to pay the fees at various stages in their school careers. Higher schooling might, and probably would, not be available. This meant that many who were able, and could have attained the higher reaches otherwise, were debarred from proceeding above the lower grades. The second point of emphasis was that there should be equal pay for equal work. The importance of this was that it would enable Africans, doing the same job as Europeans and Asians, to afford to live the same social life and to mix and exchange ideas informally. The weakness of the existing set-up at that time was the lack of informed contact between Africans and other races at all levels throughout the country. If any sort of homogeneous approach to the future was to be constructed this separation, enshrined in different racial rates of pay, must be broken down. As the struggle went on the

[1] The 'ears' of governments, special branches, security agencies, etc., receive sounds on certain wavelengths only, wavelengths that are given them. In Kenya these wavelengths related to maintenance of the existing social structure and the protection of Europeans. It is remarkable that the Kenya Security Committee was receiving only on this wavelength as late as six months before independence, although it showed that it could readily work on other wavelengths if these were given.

government reacted. The Commissioner for Labour tried to break the unity of the three associations by suggesting to the Africans that the equal pay issue was a trick by Europeans to prevent their getting any higher jobs and pointed out that in Northern Rhodesia the doctrine of equal pay had been used successfully to keep Africans out of higher jobs in the copper mines. He failed to break the unity of purpose and the confidence that had been slowly built up. The logic of his argument was, of course, that Africans were not really suitable for higher jobs, or could not perform them at the same standard as Europeans. There was an element of truth in this, in that the African had to make the daily transition from a tribal society at home to a modern society in his job. This hampered his becoming as efficient in the latter as the Europeans who were in their own environment. It was not, however, true of all. In part, in so far as it was true, the system of lower pay for Africans helped to make it so and perpetuated their position. A start needed to be made with bringing the ablest through and assimilating them to an efficient organization while such remained in Kenya. (With independence large numbers had to be promoted rapidly, whether suitable or not, and there were few Africans with long experience and an understanding of efficient organization to take charge.) As a result of this attack the European association felt it must demonstrate its good faith. By tying the proposal to other issues which the government felt obliged to heed, it was able to secure the establishment of a non-racial civil service commission to control appointments and promotions. This had equal representation of all races and was designed to secure that promotions were made regardless of race. It was, at that time, novel and unwelcome to the government, especially as its members were selected from panels of names submitted by each racial association— an attempt to avoid the suspicion which attached to government nomination. Unfortunately it was not possible to bring the higher posts within the new commission's competence and this seriously weakened its effect. This was because the administrative service was not prepared to see the posts which it regarded as its right subject to the commission. While, therefore, a step forward was taken the position of the administrative service was untouched. Into this service Europeans could enter with no qualifications, but not the other races who, if they had any qualifications, were disposed of in the technical branches of the civil service.

In 1954 the Lidbury Commission produced its report on the civil service. It received a single memorandum from all three racial associations, a remarkable enough occurrence in Kenya at that time, and ignored it. It imported from West Africa the notion of 'expatriation allowances', one of those things, like madhouses, whose name has to be changed frequently because of their nasty associations, later to become 'inducement allowances', later still 'overseas allowances', for Europeans but limited them to certain higher grades. Europeans below these grades did not receive them. Rates of pay were geared to the previous African level. Europeans ceased to enter the civil service below the top grades. The Lidbury Report introduced a new philosophy. The pattern was to be a top sector of the civil service manned mainly by expatriate Europeans, no doubt one day to be replaced by Africans, and the remainder filled by Africans and Asians. The local European was excluded. The European leaders failed to see the implications; that their children could have no place in the civil service and that its standards would be the standards of the lower African rates of pay. The future envisaged by Lidbury, and presumably supported by the Colonial Office, was of an African service controlled by expatriates and, if and when they left, an African state. Yet for the next five years the British government continued to assure Europeans of their future in Kenya and the con-

tinuance of their way of life. Both approaches were equally
wrong in principle, but the Lidbury Report was the end of
the hope of developing a mixed society in a country where
all could play their part and of making gradual change
possible instead of a sharp upheaval. At the same time the
British government appeared to be supporting the 'moderates' in Kenya and in Rhodesia, and so having it three ways.
It was possible to reach valid conclusions that Britain supported the old regime, the 'die-hard' Europeans, and the
'moderates', the non-racial society, as well as the idea of an
African state. It may well have been, however, that the third
possibility was really the only one and that the Lidbury
Report was the only realist official pronouncement in those
years. At that point the European Civil Servants' Association
gave up. It seemed pointless to work for unity any more, since
there must be increasing separation, in spite of later statements by the government about a unified civil service when,
in fact, there was no unity.[1] This story, although one of
failure and unimportant in itself, does illustrate many of the
attitudes and currents of thought that contributed to *uhuru*.
We see the hostility of the European settler to the civil service blinding him to the implications of what was happening. He was receiving his assurances and could not see the
undermining of his position in what was happening to
the civil service.[2] It was an occasion, of course, where all

[1] See Appendix.

[2] In October 1954, Lord Howick, then Governor of Kenya, in addressing the 11th Annual Agricultural Conference in Nairobi, said: 'I think
you will agree that the prospective agricultural immigrant who hopes
to work on a farm in the Highlands has several reasons for looking hope-
fully to the future. He will be coming to a country where much of what
affects him will be settled by experienced farmers now to be elected to
Production Committees. He will know that by emigrating from the
United Kingdom to Kenya he is doing something approved by the
United Kingdom Government and to be encouraged by it in the future.

'He will also know that the Secretary of State for the Colonies has

races had spoken with one voice. This probably frightened the settler more than the government, since only a minority of European settlers was able to see the country as a unity instead of a white enclave.

That, if all three races were given the same problem, they would each come up with a different solution was almost an axiom of government at that time, although it had received a rude shock in 1951. The official government then was in a minority in the Legislative Council although it had more members than the unofficial representatives of any two races. The Finance Minister was, however, able to achieve the unexpected and so to antagonize all races that they voted together and tore his budget to shreds. After that considerable care was taken to ensure an official majority overall and that the voice of the representatives of the people, if it should ever be united again, would not be able to control the situation. Indeed as long as the British government remained responsible for Kenya it could not allow this to happen. What is significant is its assumption that the races could not unite. Was it also, perhaps, a feeling that they must not unite? The other significant thing is that until internal self-government no one in Kenya had had any experience of democratic responsibility. They went through the parliamentary forms, but its essence was not there. Without the problems of responsibility all must be against the government. What is often forgotten is that the introduction of two- or multi-party political systems at independence is an entirely novel thing of which no one in the country has experience. Before then parties are pressure groups, not potential governments.

---

recently said in Nairobi that the British settler is really here to stay and has an essential part to play. Let me remind you of some of his words: "Her Majesty's Government are not likely to lend themselves to encouraging people to come if they intend to betray them. They will be entitled to feel confidence in the possession of the homes they have built or will build for themselves and for their children." '

I have referred to the minority of European settlers who saw the country as a whole. In fact they were not significant, but they serve to correct what might otherwise be an un-balanced picture of the European community. Under the able leadership of Sir Michael Blundell they even appeared for a time to be of importance.

The impact of the Emergency on European thought was considerable and gave Blundell and men like him a chance to come to the fore and speak their minds.[1] Something had obviously gone seriously wrong. African aspirations (or, perhaps, simply frustrations) had found a voice in violence and would have to be taken into account. The gradual development of a multi-racial or non-racial society seemed to offer a way out—the solution also proposed by Sir Roy Welensky in Rhodesia. The fact that the European settlers had been unable themselves to contain the Emergency but that help from Britain had been needed (even though they were not the government and had not asked for help) emphasized the weakness of their position and made them ready for an adjustment of attitudes. As, however, the Mau Mau came to be mastered, and as the British government gave more assurances about the settlers' future, the influence of

[1] Extracts from speeches of European leaders soon after the declaration of Emergency:

'The Government must realize that we are all in this together and this idea of continually working in strongly opposed racial groups is absolutely faulty', Mr Michael Blundell, 14 Jan. 1953.

'It is no good people thinking that the European can have the government of this country by himself. He can, we believe, achieve perhaps the major power, but he can only do so by associating himself with those members of other races with the ability and character to participate in it', Mr Maconochie Welwood, 22 Jan. 1953.

'I think we must ask ourselves humbly . . . what we can do to make certain that he [the African] will have a loyal place in the future, and a happy one, and can really make our partnership from something that we all pay lip-service to', Lord Portsmouth, 25 Jan. 1953. Quoted in *The Civil Service Journal*, no. 139, April 1953, p. 3.

G

this group was reduced and older attitudes re-asserted themselves. When the final change came, and independence was certain, the group was attacked for having traitorously sold the European cause when, in fact, they had provided the one hope, not of maintaining it, for of that there was no hope, but of producing a viable society with a future in it for all races. Nor did even the 'moderate' leaders see how their position had been sapped by the Lidbury Report, which pointed clearly to a civil service run by aliens until replaced by Africans. The last European settler could not be far behind the last European civil servant. The 'moderate' group appeared to gain some support from the British government, but this, as we have seen, appeared to back all solutions.

In the post-Emergency period, conscious of having failed to reduce the Mau Mau by their own strength, the European settlers began to rely, in their minds, on Rhodesia. They made positive attempts at informal relations with it. An amusing sidelight on this was the appointment of a Trade Commissioner to Rhodesia. The European settlers pressed for this and wished to send one of their own number, of standing, who would be able to keep them in touch with Europeans in Rhodesia and the Rhodesian government. The fact that Rhodesia produced similar goods to Kenya and, where she did not, was trying to do so and was strongly protectionist, robbed the appointment of any trading significance. Whether the civil servant concerned with the appointment did not understand this or whether he deliberately misunderstood it is hard to say. The settlers' proposals were not accepted and a real trade commissioner was appointed, a civil servant with no political connections. Rhodesia filled the gaps in its own production, and during his period of office, through no fault of his, trade with Rhodesia fell steadily. The idea was doomed to failure and the episode is unimportant except as indicating an increasing fear on the part of the European settler, a need to seek allies other than Britain and an increasing inclination to hold on to his old position. The approach was summed up in the phrase: 'Welensky won't (or, can't afford to) let us down.'

We have given a lot of attention to the European farmer in trying to understand the contribution of the European to *uhuru*. The civil servant generally reflected settler attitudes although not in the same proportions; more fell into the 'moderate' class. The European business man is in a different category. The minor local European business man or industrialist shared the views of the farmer, although he was less politically concerned and, like the civil servant, more inclined to 'moderation'. The representative of the large overseas firm was essentially non-political. Both were more concerned with the enhancement of business and profits. They were more adaptable. They could make considerable adjustments as the political climate changed. The foreign firms had already, in many cases, acquired experience of the kind of adjustment needed and many anticipated it. They were in the forefront of schemes for training Africans for higher positions. They combed the school-leavers in a search for talent for potential promotion.

They did this to such an extent that they made it very difficult for the government to recruit Africans of ability to its staff. The supply was scarce, and the civil service did not in the late 'fifties offer comparable attractions. This accentuated the existing differences within the civil service, since the government could only recruit the poorer quality, if it could recruit any at a reasonable standard of education at all. Thus the system by its structure widens the differences between the races and these differences then justify the structure. Because Africans are treated as inferior and paid less only inferior Africans can be recruited, thus proving that Africans are inferior. Such an argument would never be formally accepted, but it underlay much thinking about

Africans, thinking which tended to be limited to noting their inefficiency. It is noteworthy that at a later Commission of Enquiry into the Civil Service, the Fleming Commission, only one ministry made representations which took account of the recruitment problems and conditions of African lower grades. The remainder confined themselves to the higher reaches of the civil service and considered the lower satisfactory. This is because the problems of these grades are outside the range and comprehension of the senior civil servants who submit memoranda, and the Africans were unable to present their problems in terms that the senior civil servants could comprehend. Even in departmental Whitley Councils, fairly intimate affairs, the voice of the African, ill-expressed at that level when heard, was drowned by the staff side representatives of the other races. A pattern that we have seen in other fields was repeated here. It caused increasing bitterness and frustation at this level and even after independence African lower grades regarded themselves as discriminated against.

Finally we must note behaviour in daily contacts with individuals. This, as much as anything, contributed to the African's sense of lack of status. The most striking example of this was the use of Swahili as the conventional language between Europeans and Africans. It was considered offensive for an African to speak to a European in English. This meant that both had to learn another language. Swahili obviously moved up from the Coast, the only place where it is a spoken local tongue, with the Arab slave raiders and the railway. It was, at first, a convenience, since there were many tribes, including a number that did not speak a Bantu language. As time went on it became a barrier to communication and understanding, as it was imperfectly understood on both sides. While it is possible to translate simple thoughts and commands into a third language, it is not possible to catch those nuances of tone and inflexion that do so much to reveal feelings. Even when Africans returned to Kenya from education abroad many Europeans insisted on talking to them in Swahili and in replying to a polite 'How do you do?' with 'Jambo'.

As time went on the use of English by Africans became more widespread. In dealing with any but artisans and labourers it became necessary to communicate in English. Those Europeans who were deprived of the use of Swahili in making clear their different position from that of Africans adopted instead a particular tone of voice and a rough and insensitive way of speaking to them. Even after independence it was not unusual to find Africans making complaints on this score. The fact that a great many Europeans did not behave in this way did not undo the damage caused by those who did. It is natural to attribute examples of bad behaviour to the group rather than the individual, if the individual is outside your own group.

The reason for this is obscure, but the practice is common. If an individual in one's group behaves badly one says: what an unpleasant *man*, and does not associate him with others, since obviously to associate him would be to condemn oneself with one's group. If he is outside one's group one says: what a nasty African, Welshman, Jew, German, etc. This neatly absolves one from any connection with the fault and by attributing it to a member of another group suggests that one's group and oneself are beyond behaving in that way. Europeans in Africa are much given to this in speaking of Africans and there is evidence that Africans are given to it in speaking of Europeans. Many Africans behave towards other Africans if they are in a position to do so in a worse way than any European, but Africans in condemning such treatment would condemn the man, not the group. This will not apply when the African can classify the man as belonging to another tribe. It is particularly true of other tribes' approach to the Kikuyu. It is not uncommon to hear an African say, concerning some particular individual, 'No one trusts a Kikuyu.' To be fair, however, it is possible to hear a man condemn his own group, if he speaks from a position of strength. I have heard a Kikuyu, working among another tribe, say, 'The trouble with these people is that they really are honest. We Kikuyu will lie and lie to get our ends,' and his Kikuyu listeners have agreed. This is really tribal arrogance.

We can now sum up the effect of Europeans on *uhuru*. There was a positively restrictive mentality which resented African advance, as though Africans were trying to share in the heavenly banquet of the elect and had no wedding garment. This attitude condemned them to a generally inferior status, although it was accepted that they might have status in their own areas. This is not far from the South African approach prior to the restrictive legal apartheid. The Mau Mau had the effect of stimulating different thinking among Europeans based on the concept of one nation being developed and brought into the modern world under European leadership, a concept which alone held the hope of bringing Kenya into the modern world effectively. It was, however, already too late. The short period passed as security returned. The British government gave assurances that tended to support the old view and gave little positive support to the new one. Secretaries of State came and went and pursued simultaneously mutually contradictory policies. It is, perhaps, unfair to blame Secretaries of State since it is probable that a matter like the Lidbury Report, clearly pointing to future African rule through a poorly-paid and inefficient civil service, may not even have come to their notice, being regarded as a routine civil service matter. The Europeans who had formed the bulk of the support for Sir Michael Blundell were more ready to accept the idea of African rule because they regarded it simply as a change of government much as governments change in Britain after elections. Most were anxious, both in the civil service and the settler community, to do what they could to help the new African government make a sound, progressive and productive Kenya. The others, who tended to leave at, or before, independence with some rapidity had, however, caused sufficient resentment and bitterness among Africans for them to hate all Europeans as a group and, indeed, anything to do with them. Those who wanted to work with the new government, clothed, as they were, in the armour of their own good intentions, were unaware of the extent of the damage done by the others.

In a sense, then, the attitudes of most Europeans made *uhuru* necessary for Africans. They did not, however, make it necessary in any absolute sense.

THE ASIANS

The government of India in imperial times had put considerable pressure on the British government to allow Indian settlement in Kenya, but with little success. They were excluded from owning land in the 'white highlands' but were allowed to settle in a small, disputed, tribal no-man's-land at Miwani, at an altitude regarded as outside the definition of the highlands. Mostly, however, they came as craftsmen, artisans and small traders. They were skilled, and filled the lower middle ranks of the civil service and the business world. Their skills made them an effective barrier to African advancement. No matter how much training an African might receive he remained with one foot in tribal society and adapted less easily. He simply could not compete with the Asian. The latter had been brought up in a hard school, in a society with many people and much poverty. He was used to the struggle for existence and was quick-witted in the struggle. Life in African tribal society had been easier and gentler. It provided no training ground for the more ruthless modern world. Asians rarely employed or trained Africans. Their businesses tended to be tightly locked family concerns in which relatives could always be found work, but not Africans, except as labour. Asians belonged to inward-looking groups and accepted no obligations towards men in general, outside their own group. In the civil service it was a common African complaint that the Asians refused to teach and train Africans because they were afraid that Africans would take their jobs. There seems to have been some truth in this charge and it would accord with the very tight and exclusive group-consciousness of Asians. Because of this close-knitness they sub-divided themselves further, particularly into Hindus, Moslems and Goans (Christians), with further sub-divisions as well. The separation of Pakistan from India aggravated this exclusiveness. At one point Asians elected separately Hindu and Moslem representatives to the Legislative Council. It all meant very little to the other races of Kenya.

The Pakistan government appears to have had no policy for East Africa. The Indian government, after Indian independence, abandoned its rôle of protecting Indian interests in Kenya. As a country which had itself attained independence it supported the principle of independence in Kenya as a simple proposition. It seems to have assumed that it could best look after Indians in Kenya by supporting African 'nationalists' and advising the Indian community in Kenya to identify themselves with movements for independence. This was a pious and unrealistic policy, but it would be hard to say that any other would have had more or less effect. Probably no policy of the Indian government would have had any direct influence.

The policy ignored reality in that it failed to recognize that in Kenya Asians were themselves a privileged group. They were higher socially than Africans. They had status, if less than the highest. They enjoyed higher incomes and a higher standard of living than they could hope to enjoy in India. After immigration restrictions were imposed their only means of entry was by marrying Kenya Asian girls. These girls were at a premium in the Indian marriage market as they could ensure for their husbands a better job than these could get in India. When the stars were in the right conjunction Asian fathers took their daughters to India to seek a husband for them. What the Indian government was saying was: throw away your privileged position. This had no effect but ensured that Indian policy could not be criticized by Africans.

The Indian policy ignored reality, too, in not taking account of the group-exclusiveness of Asians. Marriages between Europeans and Africans are relatively commoner than marriages between Europeans and Asians. Marriages between Asians and Africans do not exist. This is not to suggest that marriage is a criterion of racial merging, but it serves as an indicator. Only rarely can the European idea of marriage based on sublimated (or even unsublimated) physical desire pierce the Asian system of arranged marriages; the African idea of marriage never. This is partly a matter of social status, partly of religion. In all communities where the family is still important as a unit marriage is the last racial barrier, since all one's kin are affected by the person whom one marries. A whole family may gain or lose status. Although pronouncements of Indian policy seem to go as far as to suggest inter-marrying, this is not the kind of mixing with which I am concerned. I am concerned only to note that Asians mix more easily with Europeans than Africans. Asian society is tightly woven and cemented by religion. Both Asians and Europeans, although their customs are widely and markedly different, can respect each others' ways and traditions. This forms a basis on which association can take place. They can almost 'talk the same language'. African tribal society is so far removed from either of these that any mixture is immensely difficult. The African who has half-emerged from his tribal background is not a European wholly nor an African wholly. It is much easier and more natural, therefore, for Asians to mix with Europeans than with Africans. Their education is generally superior to that of Africans and, at the same time, tempered and conditioned by their religious beliefs. Some Africans, who have become Christian converts (I carefully avoid the expression 'have adopted Christianity') are more easily associated with. An interesting example of the problem of mixing can be seen in the government department which, in 1951, set up a social and sports club for all its staff—at that time only Europeans and Asians. The club was a great success although its meeting place had to be on Asian terrain. The mixing, after the first occasion, was natural and unaffected. A few years later when Africans joined the staff, the social activities became more formalized and lacking in social content. Finally the club died out. It is only fair to point out that the first African members received only a fraction of the pay of their European and Asian colleagues.

There was a basic conflict between the views of the Indian government and the actual position of Asians in Kenya. The latter were confused and bewildered. They veered between a nominal adherence to the Indian government's views and retaining or enhancing their special position in Kenya. The official policy had little effect outside a small group of Indian leaders in Kenya who, themselves not faced with the problem of mixing except at the top political level and anxious to keep their political position with the African leaders, echoed the views of the Indian government. These views received little credit from Africans for their good intentions. There arose a mistrust of Asians in political matters because of their confused attitude and actions. They did not know what to do. In any case, their position as the group immediately above Africans, the one most obviously and effectively blocking African advancement, led to their being more hated than Europeans, especially as, in their inferior position to Europeans, they could not attract respect. During the negotiations between the three races over the Lidbury Commission, which led to the joint memorandum by all three civil service associations, it should be noted that the Asians were the least ready to join. They took a shorter view, pursued no principle and appeared anxious to see what gain they could obtain immediately. They were not sure whether they should align themselves with the Europeans against the Africans or vice versa. When they found the two other races working together they tried to split them. They approached the Africans directly with a view to putting up a united front against Europeans. The African reaction was one of mistrust. To quote (from memory) from an African note made after their discussions with the Asians:

The Asians want us to join with them to get rid of the Europeans. If we do this the Asians will get all the Europeans' jobs and keep us out. Of the two devils the European is the better.

This quotation is significant. It was not meant for other than African eyes and can be regarded as an unaffected expression of feeling. It showed the deep hostility of the Africans against both races, even though they might be negotiating with them in apparent amicability and mutual trust. Of this most Europeans were unaware, in spite of the Mau Mau. The Africans to whom they talked appeared friendly and, indeed, might be friendly to the individual European. It is always difficult for someone in a superior position to know what is in the mind or heart of someone in an inferior position. The interest of the latter, if not fear, governs his choice of words and dictates a friendly approach. He cannot speak from his heart and it would give an exaggerated impression if he did, since many of our deep emotions are never translated into actions. In any case, the friendly approach may be quite genuine on a personal basis. One may like an individual European and hate the race. If one is asked if one hates Europeans one will deny it, because hatred is not a sentiment that is conventionally to be admitted, and one will back up the denial (the more if it is true) by examples of Europeans one likes. This vitiates most European opinion about Africans (and, indeed, about Asians). It explains why it is unexpected when such strong undercurrents of hostility are converted into overt acts. Nor does the sentence 'Of the two devils the European is the better', impute any virtue to the European. It suggests only that he is less dangerous and offers more hope.

The Asian, then, like the European, made his contribution to *uhuru* by building up hostility against himself. He created a more effective blockage to African advancement. Being nearer to the African in the economic scale he had to emphasize his distinctness. As an entrepreneur and by his skills he made a real, but limited, contribution to the economy. From the point of view of his group as a whole he was right to see himself on the side of the privileged. Since the moves to independence the lower strata of Asians have suffered greatly in unemployment and cannot recover. African advance was bound to create this position. In a job shortage Africans will have preference. If the Asians do not have a privileged position in Kenya then they have no position. At least they have their own tightly knit family groups and their religious-cum-charitable organizations to give them some care. These Africans increasingly lack, especially as the tribal structure breaks down. Some of these charitable institutions sought to acquire European land to settle poor Asians but the hostility to the idea of Asians owning land, certainly new Asian landowners, made this impossible. (It is bad enough having European landowners. We do not want Asians buying our land as well.)

CHAPTER FOUR

The Africans

WHERE so many forces, threads, influences come to bear on anything, they affect each other at many points. Each thread cannot be considered in isolation. In discussing attitudes of Europeans and Asians we have already had to consider their effects in creating attitudes and feelings among Africans. The dominant effect is one of racial hostility but the African scene is more complex than that.

While the African is moving more and more into a market economy he is not one generation removed from subsistence agriculture and his indigenous tribal structure. There is not a single African leader in Kenya who was not himself brought up in a tribal environment and in tribal ways. These ways are instilled into his mind at an early age; at his mother's knee and in the tribal ceremonies that mark his growth. Here is his essential nurture. Here he has a place where he belongs in a well-ordered way of life that he understands. The man who leaves this, acquires an education, goes abroad, finds many advantages. He escapes the restrictiveness of local custom. He finds a degree of freedom in a new world, as the European colonist does from the conventions of England. He finds opportunity for the exercise of his talents. He is more able to be himself. While, therefore, many welcome this new world and the escape from the trammels of the old, they do not automatically slough off the tribal coat. This makes it difficult for the European to make really intimate contact with them. He can do so with half of the African, but the other half dwells in a strange world that the European cannot know. Half of the African is hidden. This is a common problem when peoples of two cultures meet. To a degree they can converse because they share a common background, but each will have abysses in his personality that the other cannot penetrate. The more the African embraces the new world the more he will tend to throw over the old and, perhaps, develop hostility to the tribe (as the frustated children of well-to-do Europeans often become Communist because they find in it a new life and a reason for casting off family restrictions). It means, however, that the educated African can communicate more easily with his own kind, as he can better understand the roots from which they both spring. It may be supposed that as the numbers of Europeans with whom he has to deal diminish, the non-European background to his personality will become more clearly dominant.

What the African rarely does, when he rejects or leaves his tribal philosophy (and he must do this as it is so clearly unsuited to the new world), is to replace it by another. He enters the new world, enjoying its freedom, but without any clear sense of direction. Some Africans become Christian converts. They must be distinguished from those who adopt Christianity because it is a means to education, medical treatment or employment, or because it seems a fashionable thing to do, a formal part of the new world. But Christianity is neutral between the new world and the tribe. It supports and opposes some features of each. There is no need for the convert to enter the new world fully. Christianity proposes restrictions or, at least, appears to do so. Some of the freedom of the new world is lost in it. In the heady freedom from the tribe now found, it, like the presence of Europeans and Asians and their attitudes, inhibits full self-expression. Socialism and Marxism provide a combination of opposition to Europeans (and Asians) with a moral purpose in the increase of the wealth of the country for the benefit of all. They provide the sense of purpose needed in this new world of freedom. They have not actually been experienced, so that their restrictions are unknown. That they have restrictions is feared.

This is interesting because there is nothing in the logic of either Marxism or Socialism that would suggest the connection with freedom, except in some ultimate sense not yet reached, or foreseeable, in any socialist country, when the state will wither away. All socialist countries are authoritarian. Although they recognize the independence of racial cultures and even, perhaps, encourage these, they do not extend this to economic or personal freedom. At this stage in Africa's history, however, socialism offers a marriage of convenience. It is in principle 'anti-imperialist' and the creed of potential allies in the struggle for freedom against what seem to be the major obstacles to it. On the other hand, socialism is idealist and has principles. If some of them seem inconvenient and contrary to freedom this presents difficulties. Hence the cry is for African Socialism; a commitment to the principle of looking after the interest of the masses while avoiding commitment to any particular method of doing so; a socialism that will not really interfere and restrict; an undogmatic socialism.

This produces endless confusion of thought. No one knows what 'African Socialism' is and any African will admit this. Not long ago the Kenya Development Committee broke up in laughter at the many interpretations put on the expression by its different members. It instructed the Treasury to prepare a paper for it on African Socialism and Planning. The Treasury prepared an excellent paper on Planning and inserted the words 'African Socialism' at certain appropriate points in it.[1] In practice references to African Socialism are

---

[1] In April 1965, the Kenya Government and Parliament adopted a 65-page statement on African Socialism (Sessional Paper No. 10). This was a pragmatic document of unexceptional principles to which no non-Marxist could take exception. It specifically eschewed 'scientific socialism'.

usually negative expressions. What someone else does that you do not like is *not* African Socialism. This is an effective smear on your opponent. The confusion of thought, however, is very common among the simpler Africans, with some elementary knowledge of Marxism, and leads to movements actually to apply some socialist principles in practice. They are puzzled when their leaders do not do so. The adoption of socialism in principle lays one open to the persuasions of foreign socialists, of a more doctrinaire or dogmatic kind, to adopt one or other of the forms that they favour; nationalization (in reserve: one must be careful about that or foreign capitalists will not supply capital); collectives (easier; they hurt no major capitalist interest), etc.; while the addition of 'African' to 'Socialism' gives one a weak defence against being pressed to do so. We must also distinguish between the more pragmatical African leaders and the lower political ranks where there seems to be a widespread acceptance of socialism. This seems to be one of the causes of the leaders paying lip-service to it.

The advantages of a moral purpose, or a moral cloak, are apparent. Everything is complex but morals give an illusion of simplicity. Ever since the Greeks started the nutshell fad—all is fire, all is water, πάντα ῥεῖ, etc.—moralists, particularly, have been trying to express the meaning of life in a few simple slogans. If they attain general adherence they open the door to a degree of ruthlessness and hypocrisy that can be advantageous. Almost any action can be justified on some moral ground or other. Only Christianity, in the West, asserts that what you are is more important than what you do.

The problem in Africa is to feed people first and then to think of the good life. The commonest phrase among African leaders is 'Man cannot live by bread alone', implying that moral imperatives or ideals come first. The quotation itself clearly puts them second, but this is ignored. It is usually used by persons, who are themselves in no danger of going hungry, to justify a course of action that is going to make others hungry. Many socialist economic policies have the advantage of ignoring sociological, economic and human facts, and of promising something for the future that justifies present hardships. African Socialism embraces the end and manages to avoid dodging some of the facts through its woolliness. It fills a moral vacuum for the African emerging from tribal customs.

This serves to explain partly why the African turns to Eastern socialism rather than Western. Western socialism as exemplified in Britain by the 'welfare state' has attractions, however impracticable the welfare state may be in Africa at its present stage of development. Having achieved the bread it seems to interpret 'Man cannot live by bread alone' as meaning he must have cake and more of it. Western socialism is, also, tainted by coming from the West, the home of 'imperialists' and 'colonialists', the general scapegoats. Nor did British socialism, when in power, have any effect on the colonies. At a time when it had responsibility for a large part of the masses of the world it did little for them. Many Europeans, even, in the colonies were disappointed in this. Instead of a new colonial policy, attention was given to federation-building in situations little predisposed to federate. Most of those dreams now lie shattered. The federation idea seems to have been a triumph of economics over sociology; a belief that large states were necessary to economic viability, without having regard to the social ties or antipathies. After these failures British socialism turned to a belief in independence, but there is nothing inherently socialist in that.

This discussion gives some idea of what faces the emergent African and of how he tries to deal with it. It concentrates attention heavily on a small but growing minority and, of course, there is an infinite variety of degree of emergence from the tribe.

The tribe is, however, still a very powerful force, although its effects are mixed. It contains strong conservative elements. The colonial administration, following the principles of indirect rule (the most economical way of governing an alien people, modelled on the prefect system of the English public school) tended to leave tribal structures unchanged, except that it introduced chiefs to tribes that had never known them. The impact of the new economic world on a tribal society quite unequipped to deal with it was ignored. Tribal structures would have to adapt themselves, or be woven into the new local government structure that was being imposed on the country. This required time. As African society began its painful adaptation to new conditions two opposing forces emerged within the tribe. These were not only the economic 'haves' and 'have-nots' but what may be termed the 'conservatives' and the 'rebels'. The conservatives tended to work with the government and, presumably, were unaware of and unprepared for the disappearance of European power. If anything they could be regarded as 'pro-European', and relied on the government to prevent violent change. The chiefs, who required government approval, would generally come from the conservative group. As tribal society split, they represented less the whole tribe, as before, than a part of it. Christians tended, because of their pacific inclinations and the association of Christianity with Europeans, to be conservative. The rebels, in turn, tended to be against the churches. This connection between the rebel, the emergent African, and anti-church feeling goes some way to explaining why he finds himself without moral purpose in the new world. The Mau Mau attempted to go back to tribal religious beliefs and distorted them to its own ends. The rebel needed a powerful emotional ally in his struggle with the conservatives. This was found in the tribal oaths. The emergent African has seen a prospect of a new world of individual freedom but it implies the break-up of the tribal structure that lies deep within him, though formally rejected. The Mau Mau was an attempt by the rebels to resolve the disequilibria caused in tribal society by the impact of the modern economy, and at the same time resolve their internal psychological ambivalence about the tribe by reforming it. The conservative elements in the Kikuyu tribe were less strong than elsewhere and were re-established by outside help, leaving the division unresolved. Conservative elements, which should not be ignored, make up a greater or lesser part of every tribe, depending largely on the availability of land to the tribe. Everywhere there were traditional tribal leaders, groups, councils, etc., exercising their natural authority, who represented the people as well as the elected representatives. They were consulted by the government in the working out of policy and in its formulation. The new African representatives were not. Now, of course, the new representatives, the elected leaders, have supplanted the old leaders and wield power through popular acclaim. But they are still tribal leaders. In Kenya voting is based on tribe and not on party, principle or policy. Which party a tribe will belong to will depend on the balance of conservative and rebel elements within it. The conservative-dominated tribes have thrown up conservative new leaders who have been able, because they are new leaders and support independence, to represent all sections of the tribe. With the Kikuyu the rebel strength was greater, and with European support for the conservative elements removed, the tribe has thrown up in its lower political ranks new 'rebel' leaders. Voting by tribes, is, however, largely because the pull of the tribe is strongest. Not only does the tribe give the individual identity but the advancement of the tribe is more important than other things. In spite of the demand for independence, most tribes would prefer to be ruled by alien strangers than by members of another tribe. They would prefer even more not to be ruled by any one else at all.

One of the pulls of the tribe lies in its provision of status. Customs allocate status, whether by family, clan or age-group. The expectations are known. Within the tribe the African can gain status. The modern economy conflicts with tribal status. Outside the tribe the African found his status blocked by Europeans and Asians. If he gained wealth outside the tribe and felt justified in claiming more status the tribal structure did not afford it. So the emergent African could find no status, no respect, either within the tribe or outside it. The tribe resented his wealth and his attempt to give himself status. All the hostility of an established society to the *nouveaux riches* was present. The West had learnt to adapt itself to the *nouveaux riches*. By the performance of certain acceptable acts they could be adopted in Britain and, if not they, their children. Tribal society, based on subsistence agriculture, could not absorb them. This was a further source of conflict within the tribe. If they could have been absorbed the emergent Africans would, no doubt, have been tribal conservatives.

When Mr Ian Smith, in Rhodesia, for example, consults the tribal chiefs and elders he is using an age-old way of finding out the feelings of the people. The proper question for the sceptic to ask is not whether they were elected on the one-man-one-vote principle, but whether the tribal societies in Rhodesia have been subject to such stresses that there will be a considerable 'rebel' element which will not be represented under the traditional system. Mr Smith is undoubtedly consulting the conservative elements and they may really represent the tribes. The future may lie with the politicians, but that future may be far away if the local disequilibria are not too great.

The new politician performs a real function in represent-

ing that part of a tribe which is not represented by the
traditional leaders. Even in the conservative-dominated
tribes he will tend to be elected. This is because the whole
system is novel and outside the representative system of the
tribe in which the conservatives are embedded. Only the
new-world African understands anything of the new system. If the cry of the election is 'independence' then that is
something that all can support, conservative or rebel. (The
tribe may recover some of the European lands.) Voting will
be on a tribal basis, so that he will gain general tribal support.
No party in Kenya went into its election with a programme
or a policy. Leaders who seek a mandate for 'independence'
and nothing more embody in that word all the hopes, frustrations, disappointments and resentments of the mass and of
individuals. Neither these nor the leaders are able to consider
the real implications of their decision. This, however, is not
the belief of the leaders who feel that, with the hand of
colonial rule removed, they, with the masses behind them, will
be able to make their country surge forward to prosperity.

Nevertheless the division between conservative elements
and 'new-world' elements (different from the 'rebel' elements in the tribe) is real and remains. It is ready to re-appear
when independence has been achieved. Even this division is
too simple a classification. The feelings and motives of both
are mixed with others that are not logically connected and
may even be logically contradictory. The conservative element is not unprogressive but judges matters by the facts
known to it. This limits its breadth but grounds it on more
reality. The new-world element suffers from an undigested
mass of impressions and attitudes derived from abroad. The
conservative element is based on the tribe, its structure and
social system, with a limited adaptation to the new world. Its
members see stability in adapting slowly and are against
violent change. It is most firmly rooted in the countryside
and in those tribes with the least economic difficulties. The

new-world element sees, or seeks for, an answer to its difficulties in rapid change and a discarding of the old. Its roots
lie in the towns and in those parts of the countryside where
economic problems are greatest and land in relation to
population least. Part of the attraction of independence,
apart from the element of race-hostility, is that it is a step
into the unknown, an unknown where all things seem
possible.

All these things do not, in themselves, necessarily lead to
independence, or to independence under an African government, although they give us an indication of some of the
forces with which an independent government will have to
contend. Many governments have, without too much difficulty, maintained their position by force and many are doing
so today. They may make concessions as they adapt to a
changing environment, attempt to ease tensions and remove
disequilibria, or simply wait until the tensions resolve themselves. They may suppress some of the forces at work and do
so effectively. Independence may be the ultimate objective,
as it was with British policy for a long time; but it is undated.
Can it not be said to be irresponsible to hand over a situation
of growing difficulty to a new and untried government?
Local troubles can be suppressed, as was the Mau Mau, without leading to revolution. Ruling classes have maintained
their position and power for centuries, providing that they
are at all adaptable and can recruit their strength from the
ruled, as in Britain. There were, admittedly, rigidities in the
colonial structure of Kenya which made this adaptation
more difficult. Colour was an obstacle to recruitment by the
ruling class from the ruled. It is important that the ruling
class ruled at secondhand, through a 'foreign' administration.
It had been unable, without outside help, to resolve internal
troubles, such as the Mau Mau. In theory this should have so
weakened it that the colonial power could have reformed it,
but this would have been pandering to, and encouraging,

violence. The ruling class had failed earlier to wrest from the alien administration the ultimate control of their own affairs. The effort to do so had been less than wholehearted because they assumed an identity of interest between the two and had not appreciated that the two interests had diverged. To some extent this was understandable in view of the reassuring noises made, and action taken, by the colonial power. But their outlook was too narrow and limited by their own problems. (In this they were like the tribal authorities.) They did not disport themselves in the world at large or at the United Nations.

All countries must have a ruling group; one that has enterprise and ideas for progress, but it must have the fear of being overthrown, or outvoted, if it is to look beyond its own interest. The ruling class in Kenya (including in it the civil service) had enterprise and imagination. They had created the country and developed it. It was going ahead rapidly. They knew how to maintain this progress and absorb many of the problems created by change. While there was by no means complete identity of interest between the ruling class and the ruled there was a great deal of it. The links with Britain, in people and capital and enterprise, were of immense value to the country. There was every reason to hope for continued progress and development; for adjustment and adaptation although at the slowest rate compatible with keeping the economic structure balanced. Independence was not necessary in the interests of the country's inhabitants nor did all the forces at play necessitate this solution at this point of time. The forces for independence were present, but not all-compelling. During and after *uhuru* they were unleashed and are now powerful—powerful enough to endanger the stability of the new state. Why did *uhuru* occur at the particular time that it did? For the answer to this we must look outside Kenya.

CHAPTER FIVE
Outside Influences

BRITAIN

Part of the influence of Britain was in the natural effect on Africans overseas of British institutions and conflicts and is a continuation of the study of the African himself.

Study in Britain is bound to lead to a revolutionary approach. For anyone coming from outside to study history, economics, politics, social welfare, the trade unions, etc., the emphasis of his thought must be on re-interpreting the things that he is studying in the context of his own country. He tries to recognize in what he is learning features common to his own circumstances. The whole of British domestic history, for example, is a story of struggle for freedom against authority. The very pageants which enshrine past authority contain the symbols of revolt, as in the slamming of the door of the Commons in the face of Black Rod at the state opening of Parliament. The fact that the richly adorned Lords no longer hold power, that there is an opposition, testify to the success of the struggle and that it is continuing. Identification with this struggle is easy. The student, even if nothing else affected him, would naturally take a left-wing approach. What would he find on the left-wing? Voices telling him to seek independence and be socialist.

The student has also arrived in Britain at a time when much re-thinking has been done over the whole range of social, political and economic thought. Accepted ways have broken down under heavy criticism at the end of the last century and in the early years of this as the result of the old ways being seen to be unsatisfactory. The last fifty years have seen a ferment such as had not been seen since the seventeenth century when, as a result of the Renaissance and the Reformation, everything established was questioned. The Industrial Revolution produced its own disequilibria. With a similar time lag to that of the Renaissance and Reformation between the intellectual upheaval and its spread downwards into action, the philosophical changes of the turn of the century, ranging from Marx's political/economic philosophy to the religious/scientific controversy and the impact of Freud, have been working themselves out in revolutionary fashion in Britain. All authority has been questioned. That they did not result in a new civil war and a new commonwealth is attributable to the more flexible political structure of today and to Parliament itself being seen as the means of effecting change rather than one of the powers in the struggle.

In the inter-war years the colonial or imperial idea was successfully promulgated and accepted generally by the colonized. To be part of the British Empire was thought of as good, and gave all its members a shadow of greatness. African women in Accra marched through the street in 1938 singing 'Rule Britannia'. The disequilibria produced by colonization had not then begun to be felt, certainly not as things that could not be resolved within the system. The early Africans educated overseas, such as Azikiwe in West Africa, had neither the local material, nor the expectation of success, on which to build up a local anti-colonial movement. Azikiwe's newspaper tried to attack the authorities whenever possible, but the public response was not there. The only election in Accra before the war that aroused any interest did so because it represented a local battle for power between the Ga Mantse and the Jamestown Mantse, a purely internal tribal struggle that unexpectedly translated itself into an election fight. The result was disputed and there was a re-election, by which time the public interest had not been sustained. A small and apparently unimportant nucleus, however, was being formed around such figures as Azikiwe, as more returned from overseas, imbued with the idea of the struggle for freedom and finding, on their return, their own paths blocked by both the colonial government and the tribal system. Individual advance was possible outside Africa but not within it, except in accordance with strict rules that effectively prevented most of it. But a new generation was being born to whom European thought was being opened and on whom it burst with the brilliance of the Renaissance. Thought in the colonies had been limited, since the European immigrants came from strata that supported established ideas.[1] To go to England was to see a new world and the struggles that were going on within it, and to find an identity of interest with Africans coming from other colonies. At that time, before the war, the 'left' in Britain (under the term 'left' I include all those working for change) was largely wrapped up in its own battles. It was largely ignorant of the colonies and not interested in them.

During the war this changed, as more went abroad and saw the colonies. The war itself brought a greater international political consciousness and began to be expressed in ideological terms. District Commissioners in Northern Rhodesia tried to explain to the people at their periodical briefing sessions what was going on in the war; who were the Nazis and why were they bad; who were the Communists and why were they good. They found it impossible to explain the Communists in any way that did not arouse acute interest in their hearers. (Few things are funnier than hearing a conservative giving a favourable exposition of Communism. They were a people who did not believe in the rich ruling the poor; who did not believe in there being rich and poor; and so on.)

At the same time the war took Africans abroad in large

[1] Even though it was creating a revolution in Africa.

numbers. They fought against Europeans and learnt that some Europeans were bad. They had of course known that some individual Europeans were bad, but they had judged them within a convention that they shared with Europeans. The image was shattered. The superior rightness of the European vanished and there was a new, still small, but growing audience to listen to the returned, educated African with his new ideas of struggling for independence and the betterment of the people.

The left in England appears to have thought that all could be made well, that the poor would cease to be poor and have a share in the wealth of the country, by a political revolution; or was independence, perhaps, an easier emotional tool? It is always easier to be against things than for them, to be negative rather than positive. To work for independence anyway appeared to be a positive thing and avoided grappling with real problems. By being against things it is possible to generate more emotion by having things to hate. A large part of the British left's effort had gone into hating the conservative rich and their traditions. One of these had been the empire and the colonies. It seems much as though the thought was that the pulling down of the old order would not be complete until the empire had been pulled down too.

The empire seems to have been merely the last of the old traditions to be swept up and away. Emotional heat could still be generated about it. It seemed natural enough for the organizations of the left to form links with the emergent Africans, to take them in hand and not merely to sponsor their views but to give them views to sponsor. Most of these views stopped short at independence and that, anyway, promised to be a long-drawn-out struggle. That the last citadel, in fact, collapsed rapidly was surprising, but arose from the re-assessment of the realities of its situation by the British right. The left in Britain shades down through all shades of pink to deep red. Nor does the redness have to be clandestine as in some countries. British organizations range into near Communist organizations and quite innocent leftists may find themselves hobnobbing with Party members, without having to wonder whether they are bringing a threat of Communism to Britain, since this is a manifest absurdity. Through these organizations, however, they do lay themselves open to absorbing unconsciously what are purely Communist ideas—unconsciously because they have no relevance to Britain itself. These ideas we shall look at further on. At this stage I only want to demonstrate how apparently innocent ideas, but with an emotional charge which is of value to many on the left, and ideas which are fundamental Communist policy, can creep in through the organizations of the British left, be adopted by them and passed on to African leaders with added strength because they are believed in and do not come directly from Communist sources, or at least appear not to do so.

During the war the Fabian Colonial Bureau was started, with the avowed purpose of finding out the facts about the colonies and helping to formulate British left policies. It started in the best Fabian tradition and sought to gain facts. Many in the colonies welcomed it hoping that facts would replace the colonial myth of the left. Its first journal was called *Empire*, which suggested no break with the past but the progressive amelioration of the conditions of the peoples of the empire within the empire, in the same way as the left sought the amelioration of the conditions of the people of Britain. It seemed reasonable to hope that the advent of a government of the left in Britain would be able to do for the colonies what it intended to do for Britain, and to make a new and reformed empire.

What it did, in fact, do was to speed up the process of economic development, quite rightly, but no more, so that the different paces of economic and social change were sharply accentuated and the disequilibria in the colonial societies increased. Fortunately, perhaps, these effects were less than they might have been. The new economic development of the left was autarkic in principle; massive, centralized, large-scale efforts which gave scant attention to the people in the colonies but treated them as statistical units in a production and consumption machine (cf. the groundnuts scheme in Tanganyika—to solve Britain's post-war fat shortage—and the Evans Report on British Honduras). It also gave scant attention to local geographical conditions, and most of these projects disappeared eventually of their own accord and from their own inherent technical weakness. It was apparent that no fundamental reforms would be made by the left in Britain. Its positive contribution to social change was in the fostering of trade unions. These quickly fell a prey to the conflict between the West and the East over the trade union movement. The Fabian Colonial Bureau appropriately changed the title of its journal from *Empire* to *Venture*. Independence might be a long way off but it was coming nearer.

Not only did the African from overseas gain contacts with organizations in Britain through which the new slogans from the East were innocently propagated, but some were able to make actual contacts with the East. There was, broadly, no difference between the views put forward by the Communists for the colonies and those put forward by the British left. Neither put forward Communism itself. Both concentrated rather on attacking 'colonialism'.

The example of independence had been set with India and Pakistan. This example demonstrated the advantages of independence. The responsibility for an impossible situation and almost insoluble problems was removed. Burdens of defence were eased. In the post-war situation of dependence on America, and with the creation of the United Nations, matters of maintaining world peace would be shared more evenly and Britain's burden eased. Britain was unable and unwilling to bear the same share as before and was anxious to devote its resources to improving its own internal position. All the calculations of economists showed that Britain, with its wartime losses of foreign capital investment earnings would be hard put to survive, without having commitments all over the world. The U.S.A. appeared to be ready in the wings, and anxious, to take over Britain's rôle. These views influenced the British right.

These new attitudes in Britain caused a concealed conflict with traditional colonial policies. We have seen how the method of indirect rule left traditional local institutions largely untouched and how on top of them was imposed a British-type local government structure. This latter was to provide the forms for dealing with the new economic situation that was being introduced. So a two-tiered system was erected; one tier indigenous to deal with traditional matters; one tier modelled on British lines to deal with the new problems. The latter was thought to give training in self-government and democratic ways and to deal with real problems that were within the compass of the people. As they advanced Africans would play a greater rôle and eventually take part in the deliberations of the central legislature. This approach was basically sound, but implied only a slow and steady approach to self-government (not necessarily to independence) as the people became more practised in the exercise of affairs. It also implied a gradual welding together of the peoples in the country into a unity.

The concept was rational and sensible, but lacked appeal. The emotional factor was ignored. Africans were being taught overseas to seek power, and they were already learning what power can be built on hate. The small matters dealt with by local authorities were uninteresting. The big ones were not only more interesting but seemed easier. Big matters are always considered in simple terms—the nutshell approach again. The more complex a matter is the more necessary it is to present it in a nutshell and the simpler then it appears to be. A lot of thinking may go into compressing a matter into a nutshell, and it can be compressed by different persons into different nutshells which are then offered for selection on some comparatively simple emotional basis. The problems of top management always appear easier than those lower down. They seem to be matters of opinion, feeling, hunch, and anyone seems as likely to solve them successfully as anyone else. In fact, the good manager is one with enough experience to tell a good nut from a bad one. This is all very well in business, but what of politics? Mature political systems protect themselves against this. On the face of things every British elector is supposed to know what policy is right for the country and to be able to choose between alternative policies. Nearly every elected member of parliament is supposed to be able to run a ministry and participate in the government of the country. The naïvety of the system is protected from absurdity by the long-established party organizations which sift the material for office and the policies, which are hammered out in debate and argument. In African countries there is not the same protection against this naïvety and all depends on the choice of a leader. Colonial administrative policy also ignored the desire for power, for freedom to make power effective, race-hostility, and the effective opposition to these forces that exists when there is a European settler community.

It is easy to point out the connections of Africans with the left in Britain, but I hope I have made clear also the connections of the Europeans with the right in Britain. All that had happened was that the Africans had found allies in Britain and were thus able to build up their strength to something nearer that of the Europeans. But neither the British right nor the British left were themselves agreed. On the extreme right were the upholders of the imperial idea, but there was a growing body that doubted the wisdom of empire. On the extreme left were the upholders of the independence idea, but there were many who felt more sympathy with their kin in the colonies.[1] The extreme left began to dominate the whole left largely because of the indifference of the moderate left to the colonies. The extreme right had, for the same reason, for a long time dominated the moderate right. What caused this to change, so that it was, in fact, the right that initiated Kenya's independence?

We have considered colonial policy and concluded that it was basically sound and in the interests of the country, hampered by the political connections between the European settler and the right, but beginning to be balanced by a similar connection between the emergent Africans and the left. We must now consider whether there was a conflict of interest between Britain herself and the colonies. Where this occurs under the colonial system, policy is considered at a different level and is affected by other considerations than the welfare of the people of the colony concerned. In fact such conflicts of interest were rare, and generally economic. Using the Bank of England as a central bank meant that interest rates in the colonies were determined by the needs of Britain and might conflict with local needs. Exchange control might attempt to distort patterns of trade, as they would have done after the war in British Honduras but for the ingenuity of a country of traditional smugglers. (As a result of a prohibition on the importation of American cigarettes one could have them delivered regularly to one's house, duty free.) In economic encounters of this kind the colony usually came off the worst.

One example of this arose when the negotiations for Britain to enter the European Economic Community began.

[1] Cf. the pre-war relationships of white trade unionists on the Northern Rhodesian copperbelt with British trade unions.

Study showed that it was in the interest of all colonies to fall in behind Britain and be associated with it in the same way that French and other dependencies were. The European Common Market comprised the biggest single industrial market in the world. Association gave a protected entry into this market against the growing production of other producers of tropical products. It offered steady prices and marketing arrangements. Representatives of all colonies were summoned to London to consider their attitude. They were given alternative approaches: (i) to associate fully on Britain's joining; (ii) to stay out but to seek 'mitigation' if their trade were damaged. The verbatim record of the discussions showed that Britain did not want to be embarrassed in her negotiations by a comet's tail of colonies, including producers of both tropical and temperate products and of industrial goods. No one was clear what 'mitigation' meant in practice, but it was obvious that there could be no mitigation unless damage were done and could be proved to have been done. As the discussion went on the colonies began to realize the advantages of association but the British emphasis on staying out remained. After the conference all colonies were asked to confirm formally that they agreed to the second alternative. All except Kenya did so, for which Kenya received a sharp reprimand. It is true that at that time the British government had not investigated the effects on the colonies of not being associated and so was ignorant of the seriousness of the colonies' interest. It is also clear that at that stage, they did not want to know, or Kenya's protest would not have had the reception that it did. Later, when Britain had collected the data, and realized the position, it made proposals for all tropical produce having admission on special terms, but this was not what the colonies were seeking.

Such clashes between the imperial power and the colonies were, however, rare and their significance can be exaggerated.

They were not the same thing as considering colonial policy on a different level altogether, and as clashes of *political* interest.

Colonial policy was wise and sound enough if other things had not supervened. It meant, however, continuing to exercise responsibility and to carry the now unpopular 'white man's burden'. It was a political embarrassment in Britain. Besides, colonial policy now began to be conducted on two different and rarely connecting levels. At the lower, ground levels the old policies went on, making their slow, and at times almost imperceptible, progress towards self-government, so that African countries would emerge with British institutions adapted to the new economic world and capable of carrying the countries forward in a stable and democratic tradition. At the upper, more rarefied, level it had now to be conducted with an eye first on the United States and secondly on the United Nations.

THE UNITED STATES

The attitude of the U.S.A. to Britain is twofold. There is a great affection for Britain as the source of the U.S.A. and of many of its institutions, including its language. At the same time there is a firm conviction that colonies are wrong in principle. American history really begins with the revolt of the American colonies. History is one of the most potent influences on the young. Most people carry through their lives the undigested historical ideas implanted in them in their early youth. History is the story of the tribe and the community. Around it are built tribal loyalties and attitudes to other tribes. It gives a people its roots and individuals a common identity, a shared heritage. In America it is especially important because of the need to construct a unity out of the amalgam of peoples that make it up. This makes it necessary to begin American history at that point and not at an earlier one. An earlier history, as a British colony, would make non-British immigrants feel alien. The fact that the War of Independence was followed by a second war with England, in which Washington was captured and the White House burnt, serves to underline the story and the wickedness of colonial powers. The fact that neither of the two wars has been made the subject of a film shows the very strong emotional content they still have. A visit to the Annapolis Naval Academy Museum seems almost to be devoted to the 'Second War with England', a war that most British children are barely aware of.

Certain conclusions follow from this. Colonies are bad. Britain wants colonies. America is the friend of colonial peoples seeking freedom. This last has particular advantages. America, as the first colony to achieve independence, can expect support in the world from newly independent countries. It can help them to recover from the effects of colonial rule. As the most advanced industrial nation it can show them how to go forward. An American party of business men visiting Kenya a few years ago told a party of Africans that when they had got rid of the British who had held them back they (America) would show them how to do things. This picture of the American as he sees himself in relation to Africa may seem over-simplified, and of course it is, but the American himself over-simplifies his attitudes. He also sees independence as a defence against Communism (although perhaps to a lesser degree today). Certainly independence plus free enterprise plus American aid are the three pillars of his defence against it in Africa.

Africans who have experienced America and its colour problems, and who are on the defensive against charity, are sceptical. They want aid, and the great and often altruistic generosity of the American people is a valuable source, but they want status and respect as well. The Communist countries sign *mutual* agreements, providing for exchanges of trade and aid. They *give* very little as aid. Although one side of the agreements may lead to nothing they give the African countries a higher status and greater self-respect than buildings or food labelled 'a gift from the U.S.A.'. This error was committed by Britain immediately after the war but later abandoned. Even when Americans come saying: we will show you how to do things when the British have gone, there is an element of patronage. It is easier to take aid from Britain, as it can be blamed for the necessity for aid, and accused of doing no more than atoning for past wrongs.

The effect of the basic American attitudes has been for pressure to be applied to Britain, in its new status of dependence on America for defence, to grant independence on a large scale. Before the war it was applied in respect of India only and could then be ignored. After the war, as America saw the need to protect the world from Communism, it was applied in respect of Africa and could no longer be ignored. In any case, was not India a successful example of the defence against Communism provided by an independent country? Here was a state which while not ideal by American standards (it had a touch of socialism) nevertheless proved the case that independence and the ideals of the free world were an effective defence. That the circumstances of India and Africa were vastly different went unobserved in the nutshell approach. The reality of American pressure on Britain was exposed some years ago in *The Economist*. A leading article was devoted to what Britain could do about its 'small islands', as the Jamaicans say. Around the world is a garland of small British dependencies, from the Falkland Islands to St Helena and Ascension Island and, on the mainland, the Gambia, apart from festoons of island dependencies in the Pacific and the Caribbean. It seemed unthinkable that they could be given independence. They were not economically viable (whatever that may really mean), and even *The Economist* hesitated at the thought of St Helena with a seat at the United Nations. But something must be done as the Americans would never countenance the continuance of British colonies. Even Jamaica and Trinidad were not, in those days, regarded as independently viable. Today even the Gambia is at the door of the United Nations. We may yet see Tristan da Cunha seated there.

The United States was, perhaps, the most potent influence for independence. Britain's vassalage was marked during the Suez affair. Each British warship in the Persian Gulf at that time was shadowed by two American warships. The outcome of the affair depended on American support, tacit or open. This was not forthcoming. American policies were based on a different line of thought: small nations, independent, protected by America and guided by her to prosperity. Under the shelter of American arms a mass of independent states could pursue their courses in peace. America would be welcomed as the revolutionary force bringing independence and would, no doubt, gain some trade thereby.[1] The tactics of the Communist powers were not fully evident at this time, nor the strength of their appeal.

The underground dialogue with America on the colonies had regard only to the wishes of the U.S. Britain's own policies for the colonies were, in effect, abandoned at that level of discussion, although they continued to be pursued in the colonies themselves up to the point when the first independence talks with any colony began.

Prior to this point the reaction had been to introduce a series of 'Constitutions'. These were really a re-arrangement of the weights given to local interests and the voicing of local opinion within the central legislature, so that Africans would be heard more relatively to Europeans. None of these 'Constitutions' abandoned ultimate power nor the overriding influence of the European settler. Were they then a

[1] Every American diplomat must be conscious of powerful, commercial pressure groups looking over his shoulder.

sham, to placate the U.S., the left in Britain and African opinion? There was probably something placatory in them, but they were also expected to train Africans in parliamentary ways and to cause them to be heard and the Europeans to listen to them. They were acceptable to the multi-racial-society groups in Kenya, as indeed they were to similar groups in Rhodesia, and there was a brief alliance between Britain and these groups. No other policies were changed. A solution to political problems was sought in changing the central political balance. The changing constitutions were accepted by part of the Europeans, on the understanding that each one was the last change for a long time. By Africans they were regarded as a stepping-stone to the next one. The multi-racial-state policies, although worthy and good in principle, had no backing in the emotions and feelings of the peoples on either side. Nor did these policies have time to establish themselves or the genuineness of their intentions. A long period would have been needed and a tremendous amount of good will (and simply, perhaps, will) on either side, if they were to work. As an attempt to make the ruling class adapt itself to change and adjust itself to the disequilibria in the state, they failed. They were accepted by Europeans with reluctance and did not come from the Europeans themselves but were imposed from outside. They had few roots in the country. They did not produce equilibrium. (Neither does independence.) The underlying strains and tensions remained, but were eased temporarily. The Swynnerton Plan might have relieved these and caused a fundamental reform, but it needed time. The two-pronged policy of economic and land reform coupled with periodic parliamentary reform might have achieved their stabilizing objective. Rising production might have provided for a rising population as successive constitutions might have provided for rising political aspirations. But this is improbable in view of the growing race-hostility and the basic opposition of the European settler to African advance.

While it is reasonable to suppose that constitution-making as well as being a serious attempt to meet Kenya's needs, was a reaction to U.S. pressure, America would presumably have been satisfied with progress at the same pace. We must look elsewhere for the final re-inforcement, the last push to independence.

THE UNITED NATIONS

Viewing it from afar, it hardly seemed possible to take the United Nations seriously. The posturings of delegates, the mud that they slung, the twist that seemed to be given to honest motives and actions, the apparent absence of reason or logic from discussions and speeches, all suggested that it might only be regarded as a place where people were allowed to relieve their emotions and let off steam. It could not be supposed that this release of emotion could lead to action. Delegates themselves seemed ordinary, sensible persons, who might well not expect what they said in public to be taken seriously.

The truth was far different—not that they do expect to be taken seriously. A new organ had been created, a new parliament, and the political game was being played on a grander scale, in a vaster arena or, perhaps, on a bigger table with higher stakes. Bigger counters were now exchanged and bargained. It might all seem remote from the individual far away tilling the soil, or perhaps having no soil to till, the man whom policy is about, but it was going to affect him a great deal.

If it is agreed that the United Nations Organization is valuable as an instrument of peace and a place where the world can establish some common standards of behaviour in international affairs, can acquire some common attitudes and motives, if, above all, it is a place where the tensions of the world can be resolved, then one must accept what goes with it: the trading of interests in the corridors and the mud-slinging in public. By the common standards that are established nations can be judged, and must accept judgment since they will judge others. Even the mud-slinging serves two useful functions. In the first place mud is slung because some country is alleged not to be behaving in accordance with some accepted, virtuous norm. In this way norms are established. Even conflicting ideologies can hammer out some common standards and appeal to a common, accepted, moral base of action. Although countries pursue their individual interests there they do so within a cloak of virtue, or at least try to. In the shadow of the bomb this has some real meaning. In the second place, the mud-slinging enables a country to polish up, as it were, the particular counters that it has in its hands and give them more exchange value. If you wish me to give up this interest then I am going to make you pay for it as dearly as I can. What happens at the United Nations is a replica on a grander scale of what happens in every democratic parliament or assembly in the world.

The United Nations is, undoubtedly, an immensely valuable institution to the world, even though its critics may be right. At this place of bargaining, talk and negotiation, where tactical positions of advantage are sought, there affairs are discussed and decisions taken which have no regard to the direct interests of the inhabitants of any country. These are not so much the decisions formally taken by the United Nations itself as the decisions taken by individual countries as they play this strange-seeming game. For anyone concerned with government at the grass roots level, concerned with the welfare of individual men and women, a visit to the United Nations is like entering some fantastic and unreal world where grotesque figures posture and utter strange sounds that seem to have little bearing on life as it is lived. The Greek gods playing with the fates of humans seem more real. The visitor quickly realizes, however, that what goes on is important. Governments, in their posturing and bargaining, take decisions about policies that affect the lives of their people. Here international policies on a wide range of matters are formulated by the nutshell approach. Here new attitudes and new slogans are forged. Here America finds a forum where it can line up countries behind 'anti-colonialism'; here the East lines them up behind 'non-alignment' (the doctrine by which countries become detached from the West). All can give nominal support to these constructions, as they can to 'peaceful co-existence', a doctrine limited to the major participants in the East *vs*. West struggle and not given any attention by minor countries. Here simplifying is carried to its farthest point. Issues of the utmost complexity become elementary formulae. These formulae are valuable until they break down under new pressures or become fossilized attitudes, since they give a sense of purpose and direction to the world among common difficulties at certain periods of time. They are not laws and no one obeys them, but they enable the organization to limit the major divergencies from them and they cause nations to try to take actions which can be argued to be more or less consistent with them. Like all generalizations these formulae leave a lot of rough edges between which the individual may be ground, cut and bruised. The bigger the formula and the wider its application the greater will be the number of individuals ground at the edges. Here in this grand market place, where the hopes and fears of peoples are traded, the fate of millions is decided in ways over which they have no control. It is, however, decided and theirs is not a blind fate of war. Errors can be seen and lessons learnt and new attitudes and formulae may evolve.

In this forum all can agree on the independence of colonies. Here East and West agreed. Even Britain agreed in

principle and France modified her principles to meet overwhelming pressures. Once the principle is accepted there is
then pressure for speed in execution. Colonies are seen by the
East as a strength of the West, something to be broken. As
more newly independent countries join the United Nations
the East finds more allies and the pressure re-doubles. For a
long time Britain held out against speed on the ground that
it was against the interests of the inhabitants of colonies. But
at some point it was decided to surrender this counter. Perhaps it was in return for something else; perhaps it had become a bad counter, in fact a counter in their opponents'
hands. The new large counter was 'democracy' or 'one-
man-one-vote'. With the British Prime Minister's 'wind of
change' speech in South Africa the change of course was
signalled. France and Belgium changed course at the same
time, Belgium, perhaps, moved too quickly, too straight-
forwardly, too simply, too literally, so that the effect of the
change on the inhabitants of the Congo became apparent
to all.

THE EAST

The influence of the East on *uhuru* can be seen first in the
'cold war' struggle, which is a global war, and the attempts
by the U.S.A. to bid for the support of the non-European
world. The American action was strengthened after the
French defeat in the Far East and it became important for
her to be ideologically pure if she were to stem Communism on a wide front. This, no doubt, led to renewed
pressures on her tainted friends, the colonial powers, and to
her own civil rights programme. The latter is necessary to
prevent the spread of Communism at home. The East
proved itself much more adept at the making of nutshells
than the West. These nutshells made an appeal to large
numbers within the West itself. They are, therefore, propa-

gated from the West as well as from the East. This is done through those who are against the established order in the West and so those with whom Africans have most contact and in whom they find their natural allies.

To the African students overseas, even in the West, the ideology of the East had some attractions, because it was opposed to their masters, the West. In Britain the left represented the same attitude. A considerable number of left-wing groups took an interest in the students and provided them with contacts with the East, as well as propagating Eastern nutshells. A wide variety of international organizations for Africa or Afro-Asia were constructed, within which further Eastern contacts were made (including trade union groups) and Eastern ideas put forward. The list of honoured guests at the Kenya independence celebrations showed the extent and variety of fairly intimate contacts with the East by African leaders. Marxism itself does not seem to have been much propagated. The emphasis was on attacking the West rather than converting to Communism. Africans were seeking, especially, freedom and dignity, the latter in the form of independence and nationalism. Nevertheless some of the practices of the East were looked at with favour, simply because they were different. An African government, wanting to show its independence, needed new policies to replace colonial ones. Colonial ones were those of the West. The only others on the market were those of the East.

Out of these contacts grew African socialism, a hesitating acceptance of socialist ideas, hesitating because they were not essential to the idea of independence, African because it must be an independent socialism. Out of them also came the policy of non-alignment, perhaps the most brilliant Eastern nutshell. It was irreproachable. It was attractive because it appeared to detach Africa from the cold war—a European affair that did not concern them—while actually bringing them into it. It seemed to offer them the chance of exploiting the cold war and gaining aid and assistance from both sides. From the point of view of the East it served to detach them from the West to a degree otherwise unlikely because of the long, historical contacts of Africa with the West.[1] It was reinforced by 'neo-colonialism' since, after independence

[1] It has been pointed out to me that this is too simple a view. The slogan of 'non-alignment' was adopted by Nehru to satisfy conflicts within his own government, some pulling to the East and some to the West, and to prevent India swinging, in an anti-imperialist reaction, into the arms of the Communists. In Kenya the slogan was adopted in a doctrinaire way (one Kenya political leader said—pre-independence— 'we would rather starve than be aligned'; he was an Asian and would not starve personally under either dispensation) from the East, and used originally by the East-inclined. In 1965, when the struggle between the East-inclined and the West-inclined was being intensified, it was used chiefly by the West-inclined, for the same purposes as Nehru used it. There is, however, a growing doctrinal conflict between the approach of the Soviet Union and that of the Chinese. The Russians are inclined to support independence movements of bourgeois leaders; the Chinese are not:

'The National Freedom Movement is one of the most important components of the world revolutionary process of the present time' (*Mirovaya ekonomika i Meždunarodnye otnoseniya*, no. 3, 1962, quoted in *The Soviet Bloc and the Developing Countries*, Verlag für Literatur und Zeitgeschehen GMBH, Hanover, 1964).

'In the first stage of the freedom revolution the task of the proletariat and its party was relatively simple, for it involved drawing a distinction between the section of the bourgeoisie taking part in the national freedom movement and the tiny handful of native wirepullers and their satellites standing aside from the struggle or directly aiding the imperialists and colonialists. The situation changes when the former colonial countries become independent. One criterion therefore for judging the reactionary or progressive attitude of the bourgeoisie is provided by its attitude towards imperialism. Another criterion is the extent to which the bourgeoisie is consistent in carrying out agrarian reforms and other social changes, the extent to which it strives to develop economic and cultural ties with socialist countries, what line it takes in questions of war and peace etc. Once the attitude of the various groups of bourgeoisie is known on all these topics, it is not difficult for a proletariat to determine which ones can be drawn on to its side in a given

the West was likely to re-establish, or simply to maintain in another form, its relations with Africa. It was no part of Communist intentions that independent Africa should become a group of Western satellites, although it was equally clear that this was in American minds, a view perhaps shared by the British. It was not unusual in the latter days to hear British civil servants say to Americans: 'Well, we will soon be ready to hand over to you.' Allied to this was the nutshell: 'No foreign bases'. With these three formulae Africa would be stripped and open to the East.

The main influence of the East, thus, came through the

situation, which forces must be neutralized and which ones must be fought against relentlessly' (ibid.).

'The state of national democracy is no state of the dictatorship of the proletariat. But with the ripening of objective and subjective pre-conditions it heralds the "non-capitalist" way of development' ('Raboceye dvižjenie v kapitalisticeskych stranach' in *Narodny Azii i Afrika*, no. 5, 1961, quoted op. cit.).

The Chinese adopt a more straightforward revolutionary approach based on race:

'They [the Chinese] spoke out against the participation of representatives of the Afro-Asian Solidarity Committee from the European Socialist countries at the third Solidarity Conference in Moshi. The leader of the Chinese delegation explained to the Soviet representatives: "The Conference does not concern whites"' (*Pravda*, 14 July 1963, quoted op. cit.).

The positive actions of the Chinese in East Africa are described by S.K.G. in the Indian *Africa Quarterly*, vol. IV, no. 4, Jan.–Mar. 1965, in which he quotes the Tunisian *Jeune Afrique* of 8 Nov. 1964:

'Chinese diplomats have established a whole network of posts, agents and "contacts" along the arc of a circle from Dar-es-Salaam to Brazzaville—northwards to Kenya and Somalia, southwards to Zambia, South Africa and Basutoland. The nerve centre of the network is the Chinese Embassy at Dar-es-Salaam. The outstanding figure is Kao Liang, the tenacious and omnipresent correspondent of the New China News Agency. He it is who makes, for the Ambassador, all the necessary soundings and serves as an intermediary between the diplomats and their African "contacts".'

West at first, and then more directly. It lay in interpretations of what independence meant. The East itself had a magnetism for African leaders because of its hostility to the colonial powers and because being associated with it gave them a way of expressing their anti-colonial feelings. Marxist doctrine, indigestible as much of it is, seems not to have been pushed positively, but Eastern ways and institutions were attractive. Marxism was used as a general background for destructive criticism of Western ideas. Direct propaganda was directed at destroying these rather than replacing them, so confusing African thinking and the African scene, and making Africa, as Mr Chou-en-Lai said, 'Ripe for revolution,' a place of divided loyalties where every idea was suspect. The rudder of the boat was removed.

I have not asked in this consideration of the influence of the East whether in the last analysis Communism may not, perhaps, be the right answer to Africa's problems. At this point it is clear that its immediate effects are harmful and destructive. Further on we shall have to consider whether, as a result of the course taken by Africa, Communism is not the right ultimate answer.

CHAPTER SIX

The Transition Period

THE first Lancaster House conference on Kenya's independence took place in January–March 1960. The second in early 1962. Internal self-government came in June 1963, independence in December 1963. The years from 1960 to 1963 are a transition period. Independence was certain and its effects were felt.

The first conference followed quickly on the British government's change of policy. Assurances to Europeans ceased to be uttered. The settlement of Europeans stopped. The colonial government set about preparing as best it could for independence, knowing that it would have less time than it needed and that that time would be further curtailed. There was no time now for evolving towards independence. Hurried attempts had to be made to provide a structure that it was hoped, not very sanguinely, would be able to look after the country in the future. As the pace grew hotter it became too fast for London, and colonial civil servants found themselves making decisions on a great range of subjects formerly referred to London, and in a situation of growing complexity. The Congo soon provided a lesson in the need for preparation. Before looking more closely at these moves there are general effects to consider.

The first effects were alarm for the future among European settlers and caution among investors. Investment, except for commitments in the pipeline, ceased. Overseas investors stated their intention of waiting for two years to see how things turned out. The Congo had been a great shock to investors who had seen nothing to worry about in the advent of an African government. The East-inspired African political hysteria over Lumumba and the campaign from the East against mercenaries tied in with the non-alignment policy and was likely to be applied to alien civil servants as opposed to 'advisers'. (It is interesting to recall that Nkrumah's first troops in the Congo were led by British 'mercenaries'.) With the cessation of overseas investment,[1] which had been a big factor in Kenya's post-war progress, unemployment on a large scale began to appear in the towns.

European farmers, uncertain of their future, ceased to develop their farms and worked them to get what they could out of them in the quickest time. They ceased to plough back their profits and they sent their money abroad. The Asian community also began to send money abroad, but to Britain rather than India. The considerable normal capital outflow was enhanced while the normally much greater capital inflow, which had masked it, dried up. This put some strain on the banking system which made considerable efforts to maintain the level of advances and to keep the economy fluid and moving. The big overseas banks operating in East Africa normally account separately for their East African business, although there is no special logic in this under the Currency Board system. This system provides for almost 100 per cent currency backing in sterling and the issue of local notes or coins in exchange for the deposit of notes or coins of an equivalent value in London. An East African Currency Board twenty shilling note is the same as a Bank of England one pound note. This had great advantages in this crisis since the commercial banks were not dependent for their money supply on a local central bank which could

[1] Between 1960 and 1961, gross fixed capital formation in agriculture fell from £5·2 m. to £4·2 m. In non-residential building and construction by private non-agricultural organizations it fell from £4 m. to £2 m. (This was only the beginning.) See T. C. I. Ryan, 'A Rejoinder to Dr Clayton's Note', *The East African Economics Review*, vol. 10, no. 1, June 1963.

not have supplied them, except by printing. If the currency had been really local the crisis would have led to currency restrictions and import controls and further brakes on the economy. With the Bank of England as Kenya's central bank this was avoided and Kenya had virtually unlimited financial resources available to its banking system. Its needs in relation to the Bank of England's resources of any currency were small. When a deposit was transferred from Kenya to London the Currency Board had full backing for it and it was the same as a transfer within one currency system. The commercial banks were able to transfer funds back to Kenya from London and allow their local advances to get well out of line with their local deposits. It seems that the position at one time was that London held sterling balances in Kenya instead of Kenya holding balances in London.

This position was not generally understood by the public and there was a fear of currency restrictions which may have speeded up the capital outflow. The real fear should have been for the time when a central bank would be established locally. Such a thing is not only one of the prestige symbols of independence but a mark of non-alignment and a protection against neo-colonialism. In any case it seems that London must, in principle, support the idea of local central banks. It would be embarrassing for it to be saddled with the currency problems and needs of the under-developed countries of the Commonwealth, which in total must be a significant amount, with the possibility in certain circumstances of having to hold funds in a whole series of potentially unstable countries instead of their having to hold sterling in London. This they must do under the local central bank system if they are to finance their trade. Currency problems are the major headache of every under-developed country and Kenya's interest lay in being tied financially to the Bank of England while expanding the Currency Board's

K

functions, even if this meant being affected by British domestic financial policies. On the other hand, independent countries can put great pressures on the banking system, and London would not relish its funds being drawn upon at will to finance governments.

As the farmers ceased farm development and exported their profits so farm employment fell. To the growing numbers of unemployed in the towns was added rural unemployment. Farm labour, which generally came from the overcrowded tribes, could not return easily to the tribal areas and be successfully absorbed. The overcrowded tribes had no more land to distribute. Where land consolidation had taken place land could no longer be distributed except by sale or inheritance. Land prices in the African consolidated areas were exceptionally high, as much as £75–£100 per acre, compared with an average of £10 in the European mixed-farming areas. As the African consolidated areas were developing fast there were some possibilities of employment on the land. These were tempered by the increasing population in those areas which had already had to absorb the returning Mau Mau detainees. They were never really re-absorbed. Misery increased. Some outlet was found by 'squatting' on European farms—i.e. finding a farm with little supervision and a place well out of sight on it, putting up a small hut and cultivating a bit of land for subsistence. Once so established eviction was difficult for the farmer. In the prevailing misery magistrates were unwilling to issue eviction orders unless the squatters had some place to which to go.

As the tempo of the transition period increased the disequilibria in the society, hitherto seemingly manageable, heightened. Farmers tried to alleviate the unemployment position by keeping on labour when there was no work for them to do. This caused bad labour relations on the farm. A few farmers more or less surrendered their farms to squatters.

Others found labour recalcitrant and unmanageable in the new mood of the country. Many found a great increase in theft of crops, stock and equipment by the squatters on nearby farms, by wandering unemployed, and even from African farming areas. This varied markedly from district to district. In some districts European farming continued unaffected. Many, however, found it very expensive to leave their farms for a day.

In the new situation trade union activity grew. Higher wages were demanded and readily conceded, as there was plenty of room for rationalizing the use of labour. Enterprises in Kenya had been large employers of labour by Western standards and often soundly so, as labour was cheap. When wages increased unemployment increased. Between 1960 and 1962, a period during which the wage bill remained stationary the number in employment was nearly halved. The trade unions directed their activity against European organizations.[1] African employers continued to pay less, as before.

Among Africans tribal feelings hardened and the protection of tribal interests, particularly land, took the chief place in their thoughts. They laid claim, as tribes, to different parts of the European areas and often to the same parts. At the beginning this claim to tribal 'spheres of influence' was not directed against Europeans so much as designed to keep other tribes out. Many of the claims were by tribes that were not pressed for land and it seemed probable that European farming could continue in those places. The Masai had formally surrendered their claim to the greater part of the European areas. As unemployment grew, however, these tribes too began to seek possession of European lands. They

[1] The Sessional Paper (No. 10 of 1965) on African Socialism states that the unions now represent only a small minority of Kenya's adult population and cannot be permitted to benefit these few at the expense of large numbers of less fortunate brothers.

seem to have felt that possession alone would secure the land for them as the government was likely to be in the hands of the more populous, overcrowded tribes.

As the general misery increased so political feelings grew and provided an outlet and escape. Those Africans who had generally supported the Europeans found that there was no longer any European influence to support. They hastened to join a party. With the release of the remaining Mau Mau detainees the country became more unstable. This did not lead to much action since all hopes now lay with an African government after independence, especially in the expectation that it would distribute land.

There was a general move by other tribes to push the Kikuyu back into their own overcrowded areas. It was feared that they would seize land in other tribes' spheres of influence. The Kikuyu, in turn, formed groups calling themselves the 'Land Freedom Army', bound together by oaths. This movement existed largely in the European areas, chiefly among squatters. It looked ominously like the last descendant of Mau Mau. In so far as it had any clear objective it seems to have been to hold the Kikuyu position in the European areas and, probably, to be ready to take over European farms. In the Kikuyu's own areas the minor political leadership passed to the ex-Mau Mau detainees who promised the free distribution of the European farm lands. This would have meant of course, a return of these lands to subsistence agriculture, the destruction of the economy and the disappearance of any hope of providing for Kenya's growing population. It could also have meant tribal warfare. No doubt it would also have solved the population problem.

The significance of what was happening was not lost on the African leaders and they knew the dangers. But they were in a difficult position. They could not denounce their followers; there were plenty of others to take over the leadership with the same cry. Perhaps rather naïvely, they thought that when independence came all would gladly fall into line behind the new government and follow its policies whatever they were. It was noticeable, after independence, how many found themselves compelled to say, and quite fruitlessly: 'Colonial rule has gone; we are the government now; there is no need any more to be against the government; it is your government and you must follow it.' The underlying problems and tensions did not change with a change of government. Rather they were added to. There was no longer the prospect in the future. Independence was here. An African government was here. Where were its fruits? The promises of the minor leaders went unredeemed and they began to form, after independence, the real opposition to the new government, rather than the officially opposed party. Oathing went on.

What became the opposition party (K.A.D.U.) was based on two things: first, the more conservative tribal elements and tribes and those which had had less contact with the world outside Kenya—their contacts were mainly with Europeans in Kenya: second, fear of the Kikuyu and, perhaps, a hope that European influence would not disappear altogether, so that they could hope for support from the European against the Kikuyu. K.A.N.U. noticeably represented the more hemmed-in, overcrowded tribes. Only the Luo and the Teita rallied behind the Kikuyu and their kin the Embu and Meru. In the first elections there were even some Kikuyu K.A.D.U. candidates. They regarded themselves as conservatives and had not realized the imminent disappearance of European influence. Nor had they realized how dominant in Kikuyu minds was anti-European feeling.

The leaders of both parties were noticeably reticent about what they proposed to do after independence. K.A.N.U., indeed, commissioned Arthur Gaitskell through the Ariel Foundation to make a report on the economy and advise them. This report, which is probably the soundest document produced on Kenya, is not in general circulation and this can be understood. Fundamentally, and stating its recommendations in the simplest terms, it recommended the continuation and intensification of colonial policies. There were no revolutions in it. If it had been formally adopted as policy it would have caused an uproar in the party. An African government must show its Africanness and do things differently. The truth is that neither party had any other post-independence plans than more of the mixture as before. They expected, however, to achieve much because the forces which had been working *against* the government at every point under their leadership would then be working *with* the government at every point under their leadership. They were deceived by the ease with which the negative and destructive force of hatred can be harnessed. The Gaitskell Report has, of course, now been buried under the exigencies of the post-independence situation.

As the transition period progressed foreign interference began to play a larger part. Foreign funds flowed in to K.A.N.U., the party likely to win. Some of this, no doubt, was a matter of keeping in with the future government and is more on a par with those in business, particularly Asians, who were persuaded to make subscriptions for fear of victimization later on. The foreign funds, however, did not go into party coffers, but into the hands of individuals, and different individuals became the disposers of funds from different countries. This, of course, made personal divisions within K.A.N.U. acute and the buying of support and votes became common. A leading politician, three months before the elections for internal self-government, who had been watching this, said: 'If I had enough money and wanted to do so, I could start a new party today and win the election in three months time.'

The effect of this foreign money was wholly evil and

disruptive. It set up powerful *foci* of differences within the governing party, each focus being in some degree a vassal of the foreign country supplying the funds. The seeds of division within the post-independence African leadership were securely planted and well watered with golden showers. The different vassals were given the power to buy support and divide counsel. The natural forces making for division were sufficient, without this reinforcement, to make unity difficult. The effect was likely to paralyse a sane appreciation of problems. All the nutshells and shibboleths of the outside world—free enterprise, non-alignment, socialism, pan-Africanism, anti-mercenaries, anti-South-Africanism—became firmly embedded in the Kenya scene. Kenya in becoming independent was already becoming dependent, but to several masters.

It is interesting to note that anti-South-Africanism is not an indigenous African growth. At one time South African technicians worked in most African countries and even Nkrumah accepted them, apparently without realizing the serious crime against modern thought that he was committing, just as he employed foreign mercenaries in his army without being worried. In fact, it seemed at one time that South Africa would be able to establish good and fruitful relationships with the independent African countries and be able to aid them. She also had the advantage of usually being able to establish better man-to-man relationships with Africans. South African white society is really egalitarian, with none of the class-consciousness that the British seem unable to shed. British people in Africa tend to regard themselves as superior and above menial work; they come to give orders; or, to go to the other extreme, they are excessively and unnaturally sociable and rather patronizingly stress that they do not think themselves any better than Africans (which they are not). South Africans outside South Africa, however, accept the conventions of the country they are in and treat men as men, and not as superiors or inferiors; nor are they unready to take their coats off and show how to do the job by doing it beside Africans. It is interesting to note that prior to the rise of 'anti-South-Africanism' many students from the rest of Africa studied at South African universities.

It is now necessary to consider what the colonial government did to prepare for independence. Once it was clear what direction the country was taking the government set about its problems of preparing for African government with imagination and speed. The doubts about Kenya's future were dispelled. The processes were accelerated as time went on and it was realized that the independence time-table would be shortened. Processes that should have taken ten or twenty years to mature were hurriedly pushed through in three. If the resultant spirit is rather raw this is not surprising.

The main problems lay in Africanization of the civil service and in the land. At the beginning of the transition period it was far from clear to what extent an African government would want to Africanize the civil service. In the first place it appeared to be accepted that locally born Europeans and Asians would receive Kenya citizenship and that other Europeans and Asians could do so. The implication was that they would be the equal of Africans. While there were very few really local European civil servants (as a result of the Lidbury Report in 1954) it was not certain how many colonial civil servants would want to stay or would be wanted by Africans. The majority of Asian civil servants were really local. The position of local Europeans was stressed by the European political leaders and in the various independence discussions. African leaders agreed that so-called 'white Africans' would have full rights. As a result what in other colonies had been called 'Africanization' of the civil service was known in Kenya as 'localization.' This, however, was largely a façade to retain the semblance of a non-racial state. It even seems that at one period the African leaders wished to demonstrate that they had not, like the South Africans, any racial prejudices. They were achieving their object of independence. There would be no room for small-mindedness in the new state. They were well aware of the need to retain both an efficient administration and the high standard of technical and research services that had been built up, if they were really to tackle the problems of the country. This had been emphasized in the Gaitskell Report. Kenya's research and technical services, together with the complex structural organization of agriculture and industry designed to press ahead with development, were probably unique in an under-developed country. The structural organization was in the hands largely of the European settlers, and had a bias towards them, but it could be modified provided the European skills and managerial ability were retained. Once the new course of events was clear, the Europeans in these organizations made rapid and serious attempts to broaden their scope so that they would be of national rather than sectional value. They were less successful in this than might have been hoped because of the basic opposition to them as European organizations. Similarly most European civil servants settled down to adapting themselves to the new conditions and looked forward to continuing their work under an African government. It was expected, and happened, that those Europeans who were too prejudiced to adapt, would leave the country. The remainder, a good majority, offered only goodwill, and a willingness to continue serving, to the new African government. Many, indeed, looked forward to new achievements as remote control from London would be removed. Meanwhile they set to with crash training programmes to try to equip Africans to take over many of the jobs that would be vacated. The size of these programmes was difficult to determine, since the number of Europeans who would leave depended on the general atmosphere in the country and on the extent to which they would be allowed to do an effective job. While a fairly large-scale promotion of inexperienced Africans to higher posts was expected, it was thought that there would be a fairly slow real handover. If there had been a longer spell of internal self-government this, no doubt, would have been the case, but such a thing would have increased tensions in the country to an unbearable degree. Too many hopes had been deferred until independence for it to be long delayed.

Certain factors were overlooked by both the African leaders and the European officials. The first was the basic race hostility. This was formed by the minor leaders as they fought for position and votes. It was further formed by foreign influences, both general as well as particular, in the argument: how can you be independent when you still have colonialists working in high positions in the government?— a valid enough argument, since the old colonial officials would have a strong bias not only towards Britain but towards capitalism. Attitudes of this kind were widespread, particularly among the minor Kikuyu leaders and people, and the Kikuyu were to take up a dominant position in the new government. Its wide spread, however, was demonstrated in a post-independence visit by a Minister together with his white heads of department to a minor (and K.A.D.U.) tribe, the Digo, at Mariakani. There, under a tree, he introduced his officials, explained what they did and how they worked as a team under him and his African Permanent Secretary. He then went on to explain the virtues of land consolidation and registration of title. The tribal leaders liked neither and then said: 'What are all these white men doing here? We thought we had a black government.' The Minister had to reply: 'But they work for me:

I am the Minister and I am black like you.' They appeared to be unimpressed by this. The incident is significant, not only for its example of race-hostility among a relatively untouched people, far from the Highlands, but subject, of course, to influences from Mombasa (and not very active hostility, simply the assumption that a new era had arrived and white faces did not belong to it) but for the difficulty in putting over the leaders' line in the face of the popular attitudes and assumptions.

The African leaders had not realized that they were not free, because they had attained independence and government, to lead the people in any direction that they chose, however correct, and that the attitudes which they had instilled into the people and which others were continuing to instil, were determinants of their own actions, and provided the limiting boundaries within which they could operate. This placed them in a difficulty. They knew the needs of the country well, but could not check the destructive avalanche that they had set moving. They made attempts to play it both ways, by making re-assuring noises towards Europeans and, at the same time, making the occasional anti-European noise to re-assure their followers that their hearts were in the right place. Sometimes this was to protect themselves from attack, sometimes it was an expression of their own feelings, made in spite of the knowledge that the Europeans were essential to the country for some time and that their confidence must be maintained.

Another factor overlooked was the great pressure generated from below for jobs held by Europeans. Africans studying overseas returned. Those with education showed considerable reluctance to go on courses as they knew that the distribution of jobs was near and that they must be at hand. The distribution of jobs meant that many comparative youngsters would attain posts at the top which they would hold for many years. Once the initial distribution had taken place the opportunities would not recur for a generation. The pressures generated in this way were overwhelming, except in purely specialist posts. The post-independence government was unable to withstand them. These pressures were complicated by the tribal struggle for the top jobs; particularly competition between the Kikuyu and Luo within the governing party. The Kikuyu political leaders and civil servants were too of a similar age group and had attended the Alliance High School, which bids fair to playing in Kenya the rôle that Eton does in England. A new old-boy-network was in being.

Mingled with these currents, but moving in the same direction, was the fact that Africans found it easier to talk to Africans. The European was alien, his attitudes were different. The different backgrounds and standards made easy communication difficult. The environment in which the game was now being played was unfamiliar to the European. Socially he moved in a relatively closed world. Previously the government gossip, by which information is passed and attitudes formed, had circulated among Europeans, with Africans on the outside, moving in a different gossip world. Now the positions were reversed, and the African gossip world became dominant, with the European gossip world on the outside. It is the inner gossip circle which carries the significant information, the attitudes of those in power. From this Europeans were excluded. The new problems of African government did not circulate among Europeans. This was carried to the length of deliberately restricting certain information and decisions from Europeans in senior positions, of a kind which would have been seen by both Europeans and Africans previously. There was clearly a lack of confidence and it is interesting to speculate whether it was a lack of confidence by Africans in Europeans or by Africans in themselves. On the one hand, they were aware that much that they were saying and thinking would be looked at askance by Europeans; on the other hand, there was the feeling that Europeans were alien and would not understand the African approach. Certainly as standards began to fall, the European, who could explain so readily why this or that must be done in the interests of the country, but who could not understand African political problems, was more and more excluded. This reached a point where there were both recorded and unrecorded Cabinet minutes, such as the one which resulted in all European Permanent Secretaries to Ministries reading in the newspapers one morning that they were out of a job. That they were not informed first suggests that the African leaders had some guilt-feelings about the action and felt unable to explain why it had become necessary when only a few months earlier they had appeared convinced of the need for European Permanent Secretaries to remain. Even the European Permanent Secretary to the Cabinet at that time appears to have been unaware of the decision. The feelings that prompted the decision are easy enough to understand: the need to have top officials that one could get into close touch with and who could interpret the ministers' and the government's policies more accurately; the need to show the world that white officials were not running the country still; the need to appease those clamouring for jobs and their political supporters; the need to show that Kenya had a real African government. The manner in which it was carried out demonstrated all the latent fears and distrust of Europeans, as well as a fear of having to argue the case out, as the Europeans could have made a strong case for staying.

It has generally been thought that if the alien expert is to be of real value to a country he should be part of the civil service of that country; should have a specific job to do; should know the country and its problems; and should have length of service and the local experience that comes from it. Temporary advisers are too remote. They come with imported ideas, often ill-adapted to the circumstances of the country that they are advising. They are not there long enough to adapt their ideas, to acquire the accumulated local knowledge; to know how to achieve results in a strange society. All this is true, but it is now equally clear that the foreigner is not acceptable as a civil servant, except for a short time, and that he will be excluded from the confidence of the government, even if he be a long-term civil servant. Technical aid must continue to be temporary advisers and in the multitude of counsellors there will be much confusion, especially if the advisers come both from the East and from the West.

The Swynnerton Plan land reform has already been described. It continued and brought increasing wealth to the areas subjected to it. The imminence of independence brought a new land reform. The European areas were opened to all races. The decision to do this was taken before the first Lancaster House conference on independence. It was apparent that changing the law would have no real effect, and that African land hunger and hostility to European land-ownership would not be appeased by that. Europeans would be unlikely to sell their land to Africans. They would risk some social unpopularity if they did. Africans were unlikely to have the money to buy European farms, nor the experience and management skill to run them.

It was, therefore, decided that the government must put some reality into the change of law. In 1960 a small settlement scheme was planned. It had regard to likely African financial resources and it took a long look at the most that Europeans would be prepared to accept in the way of African settlement. In 1960 the European settler power was still there and the speed with which it would disappear was not anticipated. The project had not only to be acceptable to European settlers but they would have to work it, in the same way that they worked everything else. The scheme provided for the settlement of 'yeoman' African farmers on holdings of around 200 acres scattered widely over the scheduled areas. It was thus intended to give these areas a small dose of African ownership which was not too great to be absorbed by the community. It was to be operated as an offshoot of the Board of Agriculture (Scheduled Areas)—the European farmers' board—and under the same chairman. It would preserve the larger-scale pattern of European agriculture and would, through the local agricultural committees and sub-committees, enable the European farmer to assist and advise the new African farmer. The economics of holdings of this size had not been closely thought out, but they were not much smaller than many European holdings. (Although a project a few years earlier to import a large number of European 'yeoman' farmers to bolster up the European community and to utilize the not-fully-developed European farm lands was quickly dropped when the social costs, in educational and other services, were taken into account.) This scheme never saw the light of day, as the rapid acceleration to independence began to change the pattern of power and needs in the country. It was realized that a scheme of this kind would make insufficient impact on African opinion, and that African opinion would be the deciding factor.

The first independence discussions had revealed the strong tribal feelings that existed. Increasing unemployment increased the demand for land. There was every reason to fear that at independence the Africans would simply move into the European farms, make farming impossible, effectively drive the Europeans out and, probably, engage in tribal fighting over disputed spheres of influence in European areas. By this time the lesson of the Congo was available.

A new settlement scheme was planned, covering (as in the first scheme) 180,000 acres of mixed-farming lands (out of some 3,000,000 acres), retaining in a modified form the 'yeoman' scheme and adding a 'peasant' scheme. The latter was intended to be on the periphery of the European areas and to be merged later with the African Reserves for administrative and other purposes, since it was assumed that peasant settlement would be similar to African land-holding in the Reserves.

The essential need was to make a demonstrable attempt to satisfy African land hunger but to maintain the European economy on which the wealth of the country was based and from which any future development must grow. The alternative was a reversion to subsistence agriculture and the destruction of all that had been built up. A future African government would then have had to start from scratch. The country would be impoverished and its people would suffer greatly. In another 20 years African agriculture might be able to take over the rôle which European agriculture had played but in the meantime the pattern of European agriculture must be retained.[1] In order to ensure this the new African settlers were required to have money and agricultural experience before they could be accepted for the scheme, to dispose of any land they might hold in the African areas and realize all their resources to provide working capital (a condition that was applied previously to officially sponsored European settlement). European farmers who wished to sell were invited to offer their farms to the Land Development and Settlement Board, and the offers were investigated, in blocks of 5,000 acres, to see if a satisfactory scheme could be devised. If the price were too high for this, it had to be reduced or there was no sale. It was hoped that by these means those Europeans who were unable to accept the idea of an African government would be

[1] In 1963 the Department of Agriculture estimated 8–10 years as the minimum time for the transfer of the mixed-farming areas only to African hands without irreparably damaging the economy.

able to get out, and this would have the advantage of removing a hostile element, likely to enhance racial animosities, and leave those Europeans who were ready to work with an African government and continue the development of the country.

This modest project got off to a slow start. It was decided, once the strength of tribal feeling was appreciated, that there must be a settlement scheme for each major tribal group with a 'sphere of influence' in the scheduled areas, whether they were in need of land or not. This put the first limits on the sellers of land. The number of Europeans pressing to leave grew as the political situation changed. When they saw the limitations of the project they attacked it as not being viable. Africans with money and experience wished to choose their own land. It was decided to drop the 'yeoman' part of the scheme and convert it to an 'assisted owner' scheme, following the pattern of the old European Agricultural Settlement Board. Under this each European farmer found his own prospective African buyers, either individuals or groups, devised his own scheme, and submitted it to the Board for approval. Soon all over the scheduled areas European farmers were submitting schemes, and the Board's staff spent the greater part of their time examining these and trying to make them fit the fairly stringent terms of the finance provided for the project by the World Bank and the Commonwealth Development Corporation, which had remained as in the original project. The project, in its final form, had, for some unaccountable reason, never been shown either to the Board or to the staff vetting schemes. Quite unacceptable schemes were approved by the Board and its staff and there was no finance available for them. On the other hand, the 'Assisted Owner' Scheme was popular. Farmers who wanted to sell and Africans who wanted to buy were able to get on with the job. All parties were kept busy. Decisions of the government

L

on who should buy and who should sell were avoided. The great weakness lay on the economic side, since Africans with little experience were taking on holdings with insufficient capital and knowledge. Many seemed likely to fail and the whole settlement project would be under a cloud. European farmers, in order to sell and get the price of their farms immediately, often gave the 'assisted owners' some of the finance that they were required to find, thus really selling their farms at a discount. On the other hand they could make up for this by charging a high price which Africans, with little understanding of the economies of farming and a great desire for land, readily accepted since they only had to re-pay it over a long period.[1] By mid-1961 it was realized that the yeoman and peasant schemes requiring the African settler to have farming experience and to contribute capital of his own, were not meeting the needs of the growing numbers of landless and unemployed. The acreage was in-creased by 170,000 and a 'high density' scheme planned for this area.

By the time of the second Lancaster House conference the great increase in unemployment had made the land pressure much greater. The time-table for independence was finally set. It was apparent that a project of this size was not going to achieve the political results sought. At the same time there was brought home to the British government the responsi-bility it had towards European settlers who had been en-couraged to go to Kenya under its assurances and with its funds. Whether there was a future for European farming or not a start must be made with getting the European settler out. There were hopes that settlement would contribute to relieving unemployment as well. A much larger project was

[1] Some of the 'assisted owners' have since been threatened with evic-tion for bad farming. Most found the burdens of managing a large-scale farm onerous and there was a general tendency for the farms so acquired to run down somewhat.

necessary, but a relatively cheaper one. Indeed, even the cheapest form, a reversion to near subsistence agriculture, was considered. Fortunately the finances of settlement saved the situation. If any of the money put out on land purchase was to be recovered, then it was necessary to establish economic holdings through which the new settlers would be able to repay. This in turn meant that they must have capital to develop their holdings, and to acquire livestock and equipment from the outgoing farmers. The million-acre 'high density' settlement project was launched in addition to the existing one. It had less than two years in which to make a significant impact on the political situation and to ensure that Kenya went into independence without the troubles over land that were feared, with its economy soundly based and with a hope of further advance. The settlement schemes in themselves were designed to advance the economy further, particularly by developing fully the under-developed parts of European farms. They were expected to increase production and employment on the land on the farms taken over by about 50 per cent over a few years, and so make an economic as well as political contribution. This would not, of course, happen where fully developed European farms were taken over.[1] For this reason plantations were excluded, as were, generally, ranch-

---

[1] It will be some time before a fair assessment of the actual results can be made, since full production is not achieved immediately.

'The larger farms—jointly financed by the World Bank and the Commonwealth Development Corporation and covering some 180,000 acres—are to provide the farmers with an annual income of subsistence plus £100 after debt repayment. On these, the record of the first 750 settlers suggests that farm output is at least 50 per cent higher than it was before settlement and all but 10 per cent of the farmers are on time with the repayment of their loans for development and land purchase. On the 970,000 acres of the so-called "high density" schemes financed by the British Government, the aim is to provide an income of subsistence plus £25 to £70 net each year. Here the experience of the first 18 months

ing areas. The project, which was to cost about £27 million, was to take five years and in that time about one-third of the European mixed-farming area would be transferred to African hands. Would this be enough to appease African land-hunger? If it were, then European farming could continue, and the future seemed reasonably assured. Or would the settlement project lead to a greater demand for land? The more successful it was economically in establishing sound holdings the more demand might be created.

A project on this scale demanded careful planning if speed was to be obtained. Staff, surveys, town planning, the purchase of land, the planning and layout of holdings, the provision of machinery and equipment, had all to be carefully timed so that they were in the right place at the right time. Otherwise there would be delays and bottlenecks. Maximum flexibility was needed to adjust to the changing political scene. This meant the abandonment of the system by which farmers offered land for sale and the feasibility of using it successfully was examined, and also of the 'assisted owner' scheme. Both of these dissipated the efforts of the staff over a wide area. The areas to be included in the project had to be established. This was necessary, too, in order that European farmers should know where they stood, and make their personal dispositions accordingly. Meanwhile the constitutional talks had reached a point where the new constitution was to have Regions with considerable powers of their own, and a Regional Boundaries Commission was set up to define these new Regions.

The difficulty was to provide an outlet for the expansion

---

gives a repayment rate of about 80 per cent and a fall from previous standards of production of some 12 per cent'—*The Times*, 12 Jan. 1965.

In fact, of course, the British government is the largest contributor to the finances of the first scheme, while the German government also contributes finance for the second.

of the Kikuyu tribe as their 'sphere of influence' in the
European areas was limited to the highly developed European farms in the south of their area and the ranching lands
to the north. How far could they be pushed westwards into
lands formerly roamed by the Masai at the turn of the century? The million-acre settlement scheme allocated to each
of the major tribal groups European land within their
'spheres of influence', and drew boundaries, which it was
hoped were fair and acceptable, between disputed spheres
of influence. It pushed the Kikuyu allocation well to the
west into the old Masai lands where there were no other
competing claims.[1] The Regional Boundaries Commission
followed its example while following the wishes of the
different tribes as to which tribes should be associated with
which in the different Regions. It is interesting to note
that no tribe was prepared to be in the same Region as the
Kikuyu, and even the Embu and Meru, who had ample
land, who had been involved with the Kikuyu in the Mau
Mau and who spoke a tongue similar to that of the Kikuyu,
chose to be in a separate Region with the Kamba. The settlement schemes set aside 40 per cent of their area for the
Kikuyu and 20 per cent for the Abaluhya. Only the Luo, of
the overcrowded tribes, had a small proportion, because
their sphere of influence in the European areas was slight
and disputed by other tribes.

The danger to success came from the Kikuyu. This was
the tribe most affected by unemployment, already overcrowded and with land consolidation and registration of
land titles completed. Here too were the returned Mau Mau
detainees, generally landless (although any rights they had
had were preserved under consolidation) who had not

[1] The Masai did, indeed, seek to have a large area set aside here for
their seven yearly circumcision ceremonies, which had continued during
European occupation, but it was impracticable to leave land unused in
the middle of Kikuyu settlement.

really been re-absorbed within the tribe. They were desti-
tute and their kin had shown great reluctance to provide for
them, as it seemed, in perpetuity. Here the first breaches in
the kinship-cum-social security system resulting from the
land revolution were most markedly to be observed. When
it became known that an addition had been made to the
Kikuyu homeland, it seemed likely that the newly unemployed would move there and effectively drive out the
European farmers before the five-year transition was
effected. In view of the tensions in the Kikuyu area the
Kikuyu leaders were approached, and they undertook to
discourage movement into the area if the schemes there
were done in three years instead of five.

The difficulty of all settlement schemes and of the whole
project is that a small number of Europeans can be bought
out, or all Europeans can be bought out. To buy out a large
number disturbs the European social and economic pattern
of living and makes more wish to go than otherwise would,
as living conditions change and life becomes more intolerable. The Regional Boundaries Commission and the settlement project ensured that nearly all European farmers in
the Regions of overcrowded tribes would be bought out.
When this became clear there was a double pressure on the
government; first, from the Europeans in those areas to be
bought out quickly, as conditions would deteriorate rapidly,
and those to be bought out at the end of the project would
already have found farming impossible; second, from the
Africans who regarded these lands as theirs, moved in, and
made farming more difficult for the Europeans. Outside
these areas and Regions earmarked for settlement pressures
were slight, and European farming continued much as
before.

In addition to the settlement schemes two other means of
changing land ownership were introduced. The Land Bank

made advances of up to 80 per cent of the value of the land to Africans who wished to buy complete, or parts of, European farms, provided they could supply the balance and sufficient working capital. This prevented the areas outside the schemes looking like miniature 'white highlands' and produced a small but growing leaven of black ownership there. At the same time the British government provided funds for buying out a fairly large number of aged and infirm European farmers; persons who had expected to end their lives farming in Kenya, but who were no longer able to supervise their farms fully, with the danger that this would lead to illegal squatting and nests of Land Freedom Army. Usually their children had already emigrated, seeing no future for *their* children in Kenya in the long term. A surprising number of these were found, particularly elderly widows in their seventies farming on their own. Apart from their own personal danger (one man was killed before being bought out and one old man of eighty, who was too infirm to be allowed to possess a gun, used to be beaten up and robbed about once a month) they were a security risk to the country, and their farms an invitation to seizing by squatters. When bought, their farms were sold cheaply on terms to African buyers. The one thing that had to be prevented, if there was to be an orderly transition from European to African ownership, if the economy was to be preserved and a reversion to subsistence agriculture avoided, was effective seizure of land by squatters. Successful squatters made farming on adjoining farms impossible through theft and robbery, if not actual damage to life and limb.

It was assumed that these additional measures would enable those Europeans not scheduled for settlement and who were unable to face the prospect of an African government to dispose of their land and leave the country. At the same time it was expected that Europeans in areas bought for settlement who wished to stay would buy farms from those who wished to go. In this way there would be a gradual change-over of European ownership until only those sympathetic to the new regime remained. This, indeed, occurred up to a few months after independence, when the prospect of obtaining a European buyer for a farm disappeared.

It is now necessary to turn back to African attitudes to settlement, and particularly to Kikuyu attitudes, since in other areas the programme proceeded smoothly. If, however, it broke down in the Kikuyu areas, this breakdown would spread to other areas and the whole object would fail. The schemes could only succeed as a whole.

The Kikuyu leaders supported the schemes, but the minor political leaders opposed them. They were themselves engaged in personal struggles for popular favour and power. Independence had not arrived and to be against the government was in principle a sure means of gaining popular support. They promised free land at independence and advised people neither to take up land on the schemes nor to pay their dues. On one scheme, all the existing farm labour, who had a prior claim to a holding, refused to take their holdings because they were told by the minor politicians not to, and they bitterly regretted it later on. Under the influence of these minor leaders there was a general unrest and feeling that at independence there would be a kind of free-for-all, when all old things would be done away with and each man could take land for himself. Nevertheless the full numbers required came forward to take up holdings. This caused some misgivings among those who refrained. Perhaps those who took them up were right? The attack on the schemes redoubled. Particularly it made life difficult for the schemes' staff.

The settlement project was particularly fortunate in having available on the spot a supply of able people, well-versed in local farming conditions, and used to administration, from whom to draw its staff. If this had not been so, the schemes would have been much more costly and could not have been mounted with such speed. This staff came from ex-farmers and ex-farm managers; Europeans who hoped to continue living in Kenya, but whose farms had been bought and who wished to see how things went before re-investing in the country. They worked with a tremendous will to ensure the success of the schemes—and a future for themselves. They became the objects of the bitterest politi-cal and personal attacks. There was some resentment at seeing bought-out farmers continuing and helping in the re-settlement of their own farms. They were accused of deliberately destroying the country. The early difficulties of the new settlers in an unfamiliar geographical and ecological area, wanting to grow maize where it will not grow, not wanting to grow unfamiliar new crops, were capitalized by the politicians and turned into a hatred of the European staff. One politician went so far as to say: 'They must want to destroy us; if you had sold the farm that you had in-tended to pass on to your children and then had the job of putting Africans on it, wouldn't you want to destroy them?'

These attacks coincided with attacks by Europeans on the schemes which seemed almost to justify the Africans' attacks. The European attacks in fact came from this same motive quoted above. There was resentment at handing over farms to Africans, at the idea that Africans, as such, could do anything but make a mess of them. This was coupled with a traditional anti-government attitude and a sense of the European's growing political impotence. The attacks endeavoured to give themselves some technical and ideological support by alleging that small-holding farming was putting the clock back at a time when all over the world efficient farming was becoming large-scale farming. The argument was generally fallacious, but it rapidly gained favour among overseas visitors from Britain.

The fallacy lay in the definition of efficiency. The impulse to larger-scale farming in the Western world is related to efficiency per man; it is also related to societies where labour is scarce and highly paid and must be replaced by machines. Machinery, to recover its cost, must operate on a large scale. But machinery has limits and it does not utilize every acre to the full efficiency. In Kenya labour is the most plentiful factor of production; it has practically no economic cost. The aim must be efficiency per acre not per man. This, given the right kind of land, such as the rich lands of the highlands, is obtained by men rather than by machines which require capital and foreign exchange. Admittedly within the Currency Board system foreign exchange was not a problem, but it would become one. In any case machinery imports had to be earned. They were only justified where they increased production by more than other methods. If human labour could increase production per acre more, then machinery imports were not justified—certainly in a situation of widespread unemployment. They meant, in fact, paying to some other country, that produced the machines, a part of the product of Kenya. Every economist who stops to think knows that the use of machinery is a deduction from, not an addition to, the national income, unless the machinery is produced within the country, and that the use of men, if the same or greater production can be obtained, increases the national income. The attacks also ignored the tremendous technical strides that had been made in Kenya in devising small-farm economic systems—the same systems that were rapidly increasing production in the African areas and bringing them into the market economy. These systems were within the managerial capacities of a great many Africans, and this is one of the keys to their success. The management decisions on large-scale farms are complicated business decisions with some nice calculations of risk and some forward forecasting of markets. European farming in Kenya had a large number of persons who could play this rôle successfully. Africans were generally too inexperienced. The fate of those farms transferred as units to Africans, either by direct purchase, by the 'assisted owner' scheme, with Land Bank assistance or through the 'compassionate' farm scheme (the name given to the scheme for the purchase and re-sale of farms of elderly and infirm Europeans) and the difficulties of a large proportion of African farmers who bought these, have amply demonstrated this. The early ones could, and did, go daily to their European neighbours for advice on what to do, but as their numbers increased and the numbers of Europeans diminished this became less possible and the large-scale African farms began to run down. It had been hoped, originally, that African farmers would graduate, as it were, from the management of smaller to larger holdings, that successful small farmers would buy larger farms, but the pace of transfer of large-scale farms outpaced this idea of gradual change. The increasing wealth of many Africans urged them to acquire larger units than they could manage, with heavy capital commitments. While therefore, European managerial skills were disappearing fast and Africans were not acquiring these skills sufficiently quickly, the maintenance of large-scale farming units was not possible. The smallholding system, within the compass of the African, was the only practicable, progressive method, while retaining Europeans in other areas as long as possible. The million-acre project had one great weakness as compared with the earlier project. It laid down no requirements of capital and experience for the new settler. Its only qualifications for entry were that they should be landless and unemployed. In fact the schemes did attract much experience, particularly in the labour previously employed on the farms settled.

With entrants from outside this was rarer. All Africans want land, but not all want to become farmers. This was expected to right itself in time by the successful settlers acquiring the holdings of the unsuccessful and the latter becoming the employees of the former. This was, perhaps, seeing things too much in European terms, and it is possible that traditional attitudes to land may re-assert themselves. There is no evidence of this yet, as under good and keen guidance the new settlers seem to be generally adapting well to economic farming, and often exceed the target incomes set them by the planners. It remains to be seen if this will continue when that guidance is removed, when the European skills that are providing it are no longer available.[1]

The European attacks on the settlement schemes were, then, misdirected and governed by emotion rather than by thought. An Italian film company even managed to get a film shot of a tractor levelling a road taken at such an angle that it appeared to be knocking down a fine house, and this was useful ammunition to those who lamented the destruction of a heritage. Large European houses did present a problem. They were used to demonstrate that the schemes were destroying capital.[2] Similarly when fencing was pulled down (if it was not it was stolen; when it was, it was re-sold to the new settlers for re-erection on the new boundaries) it was alleged to be capital destruction. There was little real capital destruction and eventually the large houses caught the eyes of the new politicians and a scheme was devised for

[1] The World Bank has recently established, at the request of the Kenya government, an agricultural development service, centred on Nairobi, through which the skills of expatriate agriculturists will be retained.

[2] The maximum price paid for a house was £1,300, or £2,500 if it was required for the purposes of a scheme. In some cases houses were much too large to bear any functional relationship to the farming enterprise. Houses were used for accommodating scheme staffs, and often damaged in the process, but to have built quarters for temporary staff would have put an unnecessary financial burden on the schemes.

setting aside a 100-acre farm around each large house and offering the lot to 'important' people. This had the advantage of committing the leaders, including many minor leaders, to the scheme, since any free distribution or seizure of land would also involve their holdings. In spite of a growing resentment amongst the people at the new large-scale African farmer, the new kulak, the new rich African, sometimes a natural envy, sometimes prompted by a diet of Marxism, it was remarkable the number of African leaders who sought these larger holdings. As they have to be paid for, however, some hostages have been given, as far as general recovery of debts under the schemes is concerned.

The European attacks were taken up on the African side, but in a different sense. The argument from large-scale agriculture is one that is fully accepted in the Communist world and is the basis of their agricultural policies. The settlement schemes were attacked because they were not in accordance with African socialism (it would be erroneous to express this criticism except as a negative) and the formation of co-operatives (meaning collectives) was advocated.

Although the approach was somewhat doctrinaire, and although one of its uses was to be a stick to beat the government and a means of confusing counsel, it produced a real response because it appeared to solve one of the problems that the settlement schemes created. Mixed tribal settlement had been thought of as possible in the earlier days or, at least, the mixing of certain tribes. As tribal feelings hardened in the transition period this clearly became impossible. With the new constitution the impossibility was enshrined in the law, and all the settlers in a Region had to be nominated by the President of that Region. In the mood of the country this meant that a tribe could only obtain holdings on schemes which lay within its own Region. To some extent the drawing of the Regional boundaries had ensured that all schemes intended for a particular tribe lay within the boundaries of that tribe's Region. It also meant, of course, that any further schemes could not provide for the over-crowded tribes, since they would have already taken up all the land available to them within their Region. At the end of the present schemes, if more were needed they would have to be of a different kind. This was not an immediate problem, although it would soon be a major one.

The immediate problem lay with the displacement from purchased farms of labour which came from another Region. The labour over a wide range of European farms within the spheres of influence of tribes not pressed for land, or in the former Masai lands, were, in the south, mainly Kikuyu and, in the north, mainly Abaluhya. They could not be given holdings and had to be uprooted and sent back to their own tribal areas. The more intact Abaluhya tribal system seemed better able to absorb its kinsmen, but there were renewed Abaluhya moves for extending their Regional boundary over a greater part of the European farms in the north. The Kikuyu, now land consolidated, were already suffering from acute population indigestion and unwilling to absorb more. The tribes in the Region in which the labour was dis-placed were determined to get rid of the Kikuyu, as indeed were the tribes in all areas where Kikuyu lived. Even the Embu, after their own land had been consolidated, evicted and drove back to the Kikuyu area Kikuyu families who had lived as *ahoy* among them all their lives. So all the other tribes took steps which could only raise the pressure in the Kikuyu kettle to bursting point.

In the prevailing distress among the Kikuyu in the Euro-pean farming areas some alleviation was obtained by the arrangements we have noted with European farmers to keep men in employment surplus to their labour needs. This caused obvious difficulties as time passed and the situation did not improve. The working labour resented the idle labour and employer/employee relations became difficult.

Gently pushed by the local tribes the Kikuyu began to move in increasing numbers to the new addition to their homeland. The government set up transit camps so that magistrates could issue eviction orders against illegal squatters and the squatters would have somewhere to go to. Arrangements were made with the Tanganyika government for the settlement of displaced Kikuyu at Mpanda. This proved a failure. The minor Kikuyu leaders regarded this as an attempt to deprive them of votes and discouraged their followers from going. Stories were passed round that it was a bad scheme and, indeed, it was poor by Kenya standards. Normally, however, the Kikuyu were willing to go anywhere there was land to work. Many detainees had remained at the ill-famed Hola irrigation scheme and were a remarkable example to other tribes there for hard work and success. But in the pre-independence mood the Kikuyu wanted and expected land near at hand. If there was a chance of getting a holding in the settlement schemes they were not going to go far away. They would be at hand when the plots were given out. If not settlement schemes, then they must be there when land was distributed freely at independence.

The President of the Central Region (Kikuyuland), chosen in June 1963, under the new constitution, found himself at the centre of this turmoil; at the head of an area developing rapidly, with its traditional system breaking down, its population overcrowded and growing, outpacing the rate of development, with increasing differences of wealth in the population, the old dispute between the landed and the landless, and a generally active and able people, many in miserable conditions, all clamouring for land. It was a position from which he could easily be unseated and his problems defied solution. He wisely dissolved his responsibility for nominating settlers among a host of local political committees, thus ensuring that they shared any political odium with him. His position was particularly insecure because the chief Kikuyu political leaders were in Nairobi. He had to suffer being introduced to a large Kikuyu gathering by the Prime Minister with the words: 'What is your name? He says he is Lucas Ngureti; he says he is President of the Central Region.' In the face of demands for land from his people he could only say 'Go to Nyandarua' (the name of the district which formed the addition to the Kikuyu homeland). The pressures for settlement in Nyandarua came not only from those in the European farming areas who had become unemployed but also from the Kikuyu homeland itself. When the settlement schemes began there had been an improvement of morale in Kikuyuland. It will be remembered that the released detainees had not been re-absorbed by the tribe. Now people began to think that these people would be given land on settlement schemes, and families began again to feed their kinsfolk. In the face of this the President and his committee decided that all must have an equal chance for settlement holdings with no preference for displaced labour even on the farms within the Kikuyu schemes. So a new lot of displaced labour arose, locally displaced, which stayed to squat illegally on the new settlers' holdings, the wives of the squatter and the settler digging up each other's crops as they were planted. As independence approached it was clear that an intensely dangerous security situation was developing in the Nyandarua district. All resources were diverted to a crash settlement programme, which settled 4,000 families in six weeks, and covered a large part of the district. At the same time the new African government told the people that they could only get land through government schemes and should not take it. The danger was averted, a danger that had seemed likely to break the schemes and to set an example that would soon have been followed by other tribes, of seizing land for nothing. It would have needed a semi-military operation to restore the position if that happened and that no African government could have faced, as its own position would have become untenable.

All this illustrates the significance of the displaced labour problem as adding fuel to an already dangerous situation. It explains why the politicians had a real reason for being attracted to an alternative solution, quite apart from foreign influences. The collective seemed to offer a way out. As envisaged, when a group of farms was bought, instead of being carefully planned and sub-divided, with town-planned villages, new roads built, soil conservation works put in, etc., they would be taken over as going concerns (this had advantages for the European farmer as he could dispose of his loose assets to the government as well as his land and fixed assets), all the labour, of whatever tribe, would be formed into a co-operative (collective), a manager would be appointed, development would continue and more people be absorbed. The advocates of the proposal had little understanding of the problems of farming and of dealing with an organization of this kind. They began every discussion like this: 'Look! you have a European farm like this with a house and farm buildings in the middle' and they would draw this sketch:

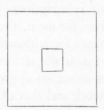

Then they went on: 'All would work under a manager and the farm would seem as before but twice or three times as many people would be employed.' It is easy to make fun of this, but they were trying, however naïvely, to grapple with a real problem. Where would the managers come from? Oh! we would make arrangements with the Europeans to pay them by instalments and they would have to undertake to stay on. That was an easy but unrealistic answer. Some Europeans might stay on in those conditions but not many. They knew the attacks that had been made on settlement staff, and they would be redoubled if Africans found their new position unchanged from their old. These could only become state farms. The 'co-operative' would be composed of people from various tribes with no common interest or background. To manage this, if it were thought to be a co-operative, would be impossible. The divisive forces within the group would be too great. To substitute African managers might remove the inherent race-hostility, but tribal hostility would take its place. The demand of the African is for land, for a piece of land of his own. He would soon discover that he had not achieved this. The minor politicians achieved some popular success with their advocacy of the co-operative, but largely because it had large promises of new wealth attached which were unfounded, and partly because it offered a short cut to obtaining land rather than going through the normal processes. They obtained support by promising land for co-operatives immediately and then, committed often by the advance collection of subscriptions, pressed hard on the government to find land for them. They were unaware that the government's finance for settlement was tied to certain kinds of scheme and that it was almost impossible to satisfy the financial sponsors on technical grounds that collectives of this kind would work and that they would get any of their money back. Nor did their supporters have the faintest comprehension of what the proposal meant. They were landless and the proposal offered them land.

I have dealt with the land settlement schemes at some length because, dealing with the matter at the heart of Kenya's problems—land, they demonstrate many of the forces at play in the community, the undercurrents at work, and how they contribute to each other; how, for example, the labour displacement problem feeds African socialism; how tribal feelings maintain the dangerous head of steam in the Kikuyu boiler; how real distress builds up into anti-European hostility. This last boiled over into resentment of the idea of Europeans who had been bought out being allowed to buy land elsewhere, and even greater resentment of the few Asians who took advantage of the opening of the European areas to buy farms. All right, if we can't get all the European lands at once, we can't, but don't let any new Europeans or Asians get them.

To give an example of the way feelings were hardening let us step forward into the immediate post-independence period. A compassionate case farm on the edge of Lake Naivasha was offered for sale. There were many African applicants for it and one European—a European who had taken out Kenya citizenship and was therefore a white African and in theory the equal of a black African. But in spite of all this play with terminology, an African is really a black one not a white one. Lake Naivasha is far from any disputed tribal area, and outside any Kikuyu sphere of influence. The white applicant occupied an adjoining farm, which had been halved in size by the rising of Lake Naivasha. He had a valuable breeding herd of national importance which he would have to disperse or transform into canned beef if he could not acquire more land. The allocation of compassionate case farms lay with a Regional committee. This committee, with an African majority, in view of the circumstances, recommended that the compassionate case farm should be sold to the European. The Region was one with no racial tensions. However, the government had laid down that Africans must have priority for these farms and only if there were no African applicants could a farm be sold to a European. The Central Land Board, which disposed of these farms on behalf of the government, felt unsure whether the European qualified as an African and referred the matter to the government. He did not in their eyes, although he did in the eyes of his own Region.

As independence approached it was notable that Kikuyu settlers, who had been rather reluctant payers earlier, in the hope that they would still get their land for nothing, made considerable efforts to pay their dues. It is clear that they, too, were now afraid of the promises of free land and were afraid that they who had participated in the government's scheme might have *their* land distributed free to others. Certainly if they did not pay their dues their claim to the land would be thin. So they did their best to establish their new title as a defence against what might happen at independence. They had noticeably changed from Kikuyu 'have-nots' to Kikuyu 'haves'.

So much for the Kikuyu. What was happening elsewhere? Away from the Kikuyu areas race hostility was less, although anti-government feeling was fairly strong in many areas. The two emotions were different. The former was generated by the educated African as he found his career blocked; as he moved into a new world, accepted many European ideas, and then found himself in a circumscribed society. It can probably be associated with the amount of secondary education, and the tribes, such as the Luo and to a lesser degree the Abaluhya, who spilled out of their overcrowded tribal areas seeking employment in the towns. We have already noted the significance of large educational establishments, such as the Alliance High School at Kikuyu, in contributing some corporate feeling to this, and by building associations between those within one tribe of similar views. Amongst groups of educated Africans of this kind some identity of attitude was being established. Anti-government feeling was a more conservative attitude. It ranged from the arch-traditionalists, such as the Masai, right through the varied tribes, and was a wish to be left alone to pursue their own ways; a desire for freedom from interference; a clinging to tradition in the face of change. When carried to extremes it turned its back on development. In other cases a tribe would be forward-looking, but wishing to change and adapt at its own pace. It had to be convinced that each step was right before it took it. Impatient European developers were not the best convincers. They knew what should be done and would try to drive a tribe on, without taking time to explain what they wanted to do and to convince the people. These attitudes will probably persist under an African government, particularly as an African government is likely to govern by directive in its pursuit of development. Regionalism gives more hope for tribal development because it places authority with the tribal leaders, but hostility to the central government will remain, and be proportionate to the government's interference in local affairs.

As the transition period moved on and widespread settlement schemes were developed, these proved popular. They were soundly based and attractive. They offered solutions to local problems and the settlement authorities were careful to work closely with the local political leaders and others in planning and setting up schemes. As the attractions of the schemes became more evident they gained more local support; they fitted in with the tribe's responsibility for providing land for its members; they gave local leaders some positive power for beneficial local action which was traditionally acceptable, although the form was new. The contact of these leaders with foreign, disruptive influences was slight and, away from the heady atmosphere of the capital, both parties, the authorities and the leaders, were able to make a constructive approach and help each other. Out of this, however, instead of appeasement of land hunger, a new desire for land grew with the opportunity of getting it.

By the time independence arrived, all tribes were seeking more land, and trying to get more settlement schemes. They also wanted to establish their claim to possession against other tribes by actual occupation. In the background was the fear that a Kikuyu dominated government would, in fact, put Kikuyu on these lands. So the demand for European land grew rather than diminished. Without the fear of the Kikuyu and one other factor, which we must now consider, it might have stabilized or diminished, at least among the uncrowded tribes.

Why was the co-operation given by local political leaders of other tribes[1] not given by local Kikuyu politicians? There were some co-operative local Kikuyu politicians, but the majority were intensely hostile. Part of this can be attributed to their anti-European feeling, aggravated by the Mau Mau and by periods in detention. Part can be attributed to the general ferment in the Kikuyu area, which ante-dated Mau Mau, and arose from the breakdown of the tribal structure, the division into landed and landless classes, which, in turn, was made more explicit by land consolidation. The Kikuyu tribe was the subject of an intense internal struggle, which had already erupted in the Mau Mau, made easier by the lack of any traditional authoritative structure in the tribe, and the whole aggravated by the increasing population, the increasing wealth of many and the increasing impoverishment of more. This was exemplified by the not uncommon appearance of two K.A.N.U. party offices in Kikuyu areas, virtually one for the 'haves' and one for the 'have-nots', although this over-simplifies the distinction. The growth of the K.A.N.U. youth wing, a party para-military organiza-

---

[1] There is a rather uncertain distinction between local political leaders in the case of other tribes, and minor politicians among the Kikuyu, since the main Kikuyu leaders were at the centre. There is also a distinction between the actual local leaders, accepted as such, and those who had entered into political activity in an attempt to supplant them.

tion of the unemployed and landless, gave a semblance of party discipline and an organ of intimidation to one side. To try to curb and control this youth wing was one of the early actions of the independent Kenya government. In this ferment there was opportunity, for power, for position, for wealth. The opportunity fell to those who were most successful in arousing hatred or channelling the distress of the people into hatred. Minor political leaders jostled for position by these means. They fed on suspicion and created suspicion. The easiest target was the European. European settlement staff were harried with accusations. If a tractor was transferred from one scheme to another, or a pump was sent for repair, it was not long before a local politician had whispered to the minister that the European in charge had sold it and pocketed the money; a succession of enquiries would ensue to satisfy the minister. If a crop on a farm was too poor to bear the cost of harvesting, or heavy rain made harvesting impossible, the European in charge would be accused of wasting government money by not reaping, and the whispers would again go to the minister and be circulated around the district. It was not usually difficult to identify the whisperer and to tackle him about it. His answers would show a mixture of currying for favour by hoping to expose or suggest European delinquencies for which there was a ready audience, and of fear of the people at home if he did not do something. One said: 'They will kill me if I do not report this.' The accusations were universally unfounded, but were symptomatic of the general state of affairs. When a European, who had been exculpated fully after an enquiry of this kind, resigned in disgust, the politician who first raised the matter went round his area saying: 'I got so and so sacked.'

Quite apart from this exploitation of the general distress and resentment there arose from the struggle for position the out-bidding technique. We have already seen this in the promises of free land at independence, a promise never given by the top leaders, although the masses were unaware of this. Now a new out-bidding arose among those who had not obtained office, and this spread outside the Kikuyu tribe. The unsuccessful, or less successful, politician appealed to the tribe for leadership by complaining about the little land that the successful leader had obtained for the tribe. The fact that the allocation of settlement schemes by tribe was decided, in the beginning, by a Cabinet sub-committee of both parties and, later, by the Central Land Board, composed of a representative of each Region and one of the central government, meant little to the people, nor did they realize that no one person could achieve any more for them than their present leader had done. The man who bid for tribal leadership by saying he would give them more was likely to win their support. So the ferment was likely and able to spread in an atmosphere of mass ignorance of the real position and the complexities of the constitutional arrangements as a result of the efforts of either unscrupulous out-bidders or of those out-bidders who also did not understand the position. Political success appeared to lie in working up grievances and hatreds. Sometimes this was hard work. But if one did not remain at the centre of one's local grievance-making one was liable to lose one's place to someone else. There was plenty of discontent to work on, but most of the real problems were only capable of long-term solutions. Political success hung on translating the feelings and difficulties of the people into something simple and immediate, which could be done, which you could show you had achieved, even if it made no contribution to the real problem, or even hindered its solution.

An example of this was given by the leader of the Teita-Taveta tribes, when he arranged a demonstration for the government of their grievances. The tribes have real problems which admit of no easy or ready solution, but it was necessary to obtain some simple, visible results. The demonstration showed:

(i) a break-pressure tank of the pipeline which carried Mombasa's water supply through the National Park to the north of the Teita Hills; it overflowed in a rather thin stream; the National Parks authorities refused to let the people water their cattle there (which people? where did they keep their cattle?);

(ii) an ancient drain over-run by the National Parks road, alleged at one time to have carried water for cattle; an indentation in the ground was barely visible, as were half a dozen men who had been assembled to vouch for it;

(iii) perhaps a dozen illegal squatters on a vast sisal state, because the National Parks authorities would not let them use the Parks land; (but they did not use land which was no worse than Parks land to the south).

None of these matters had any real relevance to the problems of the Teita-Taveta peoples, and they were laughable when compared with the problems in other parts of the country. Their importance is in revealing the need to work up grievances and to have a target, in this case the National Parks. One can only assume that some lesser leader had started to bid up these matters.

As a result of the need to replace departing Europeans, great efforts were made to equip Africans with technical and other qualifications. This was done both locally and by sending them abroad, chiefly to Britain. In the immediate pre-independence and post-independence period, however, shoals of Africans, often scholastically ill-equipped for the task, were flown to universities in America and in the East. These 'scholarships' were largely within the personal patronage of individual political leaders. It is difficult to see what intrinsic value such education could have. In America the scale of things is so vast that one slice of a subject is a full-time matter, whereas what is needed in Africa is jacks-of-all-trades, or at least a variety of connected trades.

Education in the East seems even more strange in view of the language difficulties. One can only assume that these flights of 'scholars' were intended to turn them into, not Communists or Capitalists, but into good pro-Communists and pro-Capitalists. The scandal of the American flights caused American educational authorities to intervene and arrangements were made for all candidates to be sifted through the official Kenya government machinery for all scholarships. This did not prevent a politician turning off an aeroplane fifty students so selected for study in Bulgaria and replacing them with fifty of his own choosing, to the embarrassment of the African Minister for Education who had to accept the position.

The picture that emerges from this is one of a scene being rendered increasingly chaotic by the advent of democracy, a not uncommon post-revolutionary phase. In such a society, where there is no accepted structure or common approach, where every idea is as good as any other, there can be little common purposeful action. All, or rather more than all, has been promised for independence. It cannot be delivered. The country is full of persons ready to say that they will deliver the goods. Foreign influences are at play with new ideas, fresh nostrums. Independence itself has worsened the economic situation. It is known how to deal with the country's problems, but the solutions are long-term. Ready-made solutions from abroad sound attractive. A thousand influences are at work to disrupt and destroy. It is necessary to canalize these energies, control them and let them operate only under supervision. The one-party state is inevitable.

CHAPTER SEVEN

Post-Independence

Before taking looks of this kind at the future, we must try to summarize some of the forces at play on the post-independence scene, and particularly some new attitudes that emerge with independence.

In looking at the transitional period, we have seen how rapidly the balance of political strength changed and how quickly the economy deteriorated. An African government would start the battle for development from a point well behind that at which the economy had reached under colonial rule. All the internal disequilibria caused by the advent of the European and a money economy to Africa were increased many times until the structure was visibly wavering in the balance and could, conceivably, be tipped in any direction. As Mr Chou-en-Lai said: 'Africa is ripe for revolution.' The invisible umbilical cord connecting Kenya with Britain, and through which it was fed with capital and skills and entrepreneurial ability, which flowed easily in both directions, was being broken, and the system was showing itself unable to digest the skills left and was ejecting them. Indeed their presence in Kenya had depended on two things, the existence of the umbilical cord, and their own number. In a way this applied to both capital and skill. Capital flowed in more easily, when it could be as easily repatriated. This is still the pattern, but the threat of a central bank and, in the prevailing economic disequilibrium, exchange restrictions loom ahead. Skill flowed in easily as required, and tended to stay, to be absorbed by the body under colonial rule. The more that came, the more that was absorbed, the more there was available and likely to come.

There seemed to be sufficient available for all the development that could be done. The converse was also true. The more that drained away, the more would drain away and the less would come. The continuity in experience and the combination of skills and experience would be lost. New skills could be obtained, but more expensively, with less interest in the country itself, without experience of it and often with more interest in other matters. In encouraging Africans to dispose of British skills, other countries were offering different skills, but skills that had no long-term interest in the future of the economy. Their main interest was in perpetuating ideologies, from private enterprise to socialism, and establishing or maintaining foreign spheres of influence which were bound to compete; Kenya, following divergent policies, would lose direction and flounder. Those who knew the country and its problems would be replaced by those who did not and who were interested in other things. The African leaders were persuaded to think that they would be able to play off the West against the East, and reap the maximum benefit for their country. What, of course, they were doing was surrendering their country to the play of forces that they could not control. Capital would, indeed, come in under the new set-up, but it would come on its own conditions and where the giver wanted it to come, in the spectacular and the dramatic rather than the sound.

There was a marked difference between the interests of the U.S.A. and the Communist countries in this. The U.S.A.'s interest lay in a stable environment; the Communist interest was in a chaotic environment. Free enterprise, as a development mechanism, requires an orderly environment, a respect for law, and an acceptance of its own conventions. Communist interest lay in disrupting all these things until it was able to seize some key position and pursue its own positive policies, rather than the negative ones that make up its forward line. Hence America finds itself always supporting authority, often bad and corrupt authority, while Communism thrives on chaos, disruption and discontent. The object of Communist policy must be to create these. American policy was to break up the British empire into orderly, democratic, independent states, in which free enterprise could flourish as a bastion against Communism and an instrument of development with American aid. The policy overlooked:

(a) the economic effects of independence itself; especially hasty independence;

(b) the fact that independence would release in these countries Communist forces which would actively try to disrupt society, policy and development;

(c) that Communist ideas would be sympathetically received by Africans because they were associated with the voice of the oppressed against the oppressor; they still reflected the rising of the masses in Russia, China, etc.; and because America was associated in the minds of the world with Britain, as a capitalist power.

America would be bound to support the government, while the Communists could activate the forces against it. As the underlying forces were not changed by independence, but were themselves more active, as the economy deteriorated, as old tribal forces were released with the removal of colonial rule and new ones created to fill the vacuum, the odds were strongly in favour of the Communists. The Americans were also superior white men, and their black men were no more acceptable. Indeed, superior black men were almost worse. As between the Russians and the Chinese, the odds are on the Chinese for the same reasons. (And the Russians, too, are almost playing along with the West, aren't they, in spite of what they may say?)

Of our original influences, then, the economy—the raw material—is worse and more conducive to disruption and more liable to breakdown or decay. The foreign influences are strong, as they bid against each other, not only in aid and ideas, but in cash going into the political machines. The plural is used advisedly because not only does Communist money go to the more disruptive politicians within the government, but it now goes to opposition politicians as well. Previously the official opposition represented essentially conservative views and, once independence was achieved and it could not hope to win power, was a natural ally of the leaders in the government, while the real opposition lay within the ruling party, where personal ambition and foreign money could play their most disruptive part in securing disunion and the lack of a coherent and progressive policy.[1] Now, however, there is a genuinely disruptive element among the opposition.

In this connection, it is interesting to note what was happening in the always relatively peaceful Coastal Strip. At the beginning we noted some of the forces at play there, and also that they were not as well marked as elsewhere. Now, with positive encouragement by African leaders, the Africans were squatting in large numbers on alienated land, and the administrative machinery was being told to take no action against them. At the same time the central government was being pressed to legalize this squatting. Here was a force, prompted by foreign funds, influenced by its proximity to Zanzibar, working towards the same ends as the minor politicians in the Kikuyu lands, but the one group in the official opposition, the other in the government party. If either were successful there would be a breakdown of law

[1] 'Mr Joseph [sic] Angaine, the Kenya Minister for Lands and Settlement today denounced "communist infiltration" in Kenya and alleged that money was pouring into the country to corrupt and subvert the Government. . . . Some of the country's leaders were being enticed into "vicious circles to topple the Government" he said. . . . He is the third Minister to attack extremists in the past three days'—*The Times*, 13 April 1965.

and order, the seizure of land and the destruction of the economy. The opposition party, too, played in the constitutional talks the rôle of the upholders of the sanctity of law and of land titles. It would, indeed, be ironic if they were to spark off at the Coast a breakdown in these. This kind of activity does serve to illustrate the real alliance of forces, both within and without the country, rather than the formal ones that appear in Parliament. It is these same disruptive forces that work with the natural seeking for the jobs of Europeans, to Africanize the civil service and remove those Europeans who are likely to try to maintain order, stability and good government, and who have the experience to know what this means. At each point the natural forces at work are seized and channelled to further some different purpose.

This is aided by a certain naïvety with which the African leaders appeared to regard the future after independence, a naïvety which seems to have been shared by the Americans. Africans grew up in a well-ordered society, and those who went abroad went usually to a well-ordered society. The latter would be a democratic one, the former formally autocratic but, in practice, allowing a great deal of personal and political freedom. Of the real business of governing they were largely unaware. The application of physical force in government was regarded with distaste, as it is by those elements with whom they mixed most in democratic countries. The same was not altogether true of the application of force against governments. The sanctity of the law is generally accepted in Western society, and political action is designed to change the law and not destroy it. The key to the working of democratic countries is respect for the law, and the successful deployment of the force needed to maintain that respect. The greater the respect, the lesser the force needed to uphold it. Although individual district commissioners might from time to time sidestep the law in the interest of maintaining order in their district, in those areas where a separate judiciary and magisterial system operated the law was scrupulously observed, even when it worked against the government. There seems to have been a general assumption by African leaders that when they took over the government things would go on as before. The government machinery would continue with the same efficiency, and Cabinet decisions would be translated automatically into action. They were, of course, aware that the whole trend of thinking, both of the people and of themselves, had been 'against the government', but they expected the advent of black men to office in some magical way to change this; that the people would swing behind them and they would be able to lead them to great things. Almost immediately they ran into difficulties. There were things that they wanted to do, but which were against the law, and they felt frustrated. The obvious process of changing the law was difficult, both because to do so might shake the confidence of foreign investors and also expose them to having to defend what they wished to do in public. There began to grow up a dual system which seemed to answer this problem. On the one hand the law was maintained and the official picture appeared sound and satisfactory to any enquirer. On the other hand were political pressures, either through rousing popular opinion or by other means, to achieve ends which were incompatible with the law. Under the law a European or Asian might not be compelled to sell his farm, but life could be made so uncomfortable for him that he did. Under the law all citizens might be equal, but the administrative machine could make distinctions. There thus began to grow up two ideas about the country, the one enshrined in the law; the other enshrined in the political world. There began to be a disregard for the law when positive action was required and a tendency to use other means when the law conflicted with the purpose rather than change the law and admit the change of purpose. It was a difficult situation. Pressures from below required action incompatible with the law, actions leading to insecurity of person and property, while the leaders were well aware that to change the law would destroy confidence in the country. The steam must be taken out of the pressure but the law must be kept. One thus had the spectacle of the government being ready to take decisions which sidestepped its own laws. The importance of the law as the dispenser of freedom was not understood and, indeed, the law is always suspect because it appears to favour the rich and powerful, although in fact it does so to a much less degree than the absence of law.

With the double approach to the law went an ignorance of the need for force to maintain it and the need to support the forces of law and order. There seems to have been a feeling that popular democracy would achieve this and also greater ends, that the leader addressing his followers would be able to achieve results better, and for a very short spell this was true, until it became apparent that the leader could not offer more than the colonial rulers.

It was also assumed that decisions were the same as actions, but it soon became apparent that, as the administrative machine was weakened by the disappearance of experienced Europeans, not only was the Cabinet badly advised but, perhaps to some extent for that reason, its decisions were not necessarily carried out. Among the African administrators, on the other hand, was a belief that a Cabinet decision, by the mere fact of being taken, had somehow solved a problem, without appreciating the need to make it effective by positive action; as though a Cabinet decision in some magical way became known to the people and an expression of their own will. Only too often an African administrator would say: 'You needn't worry any more about that; the Cabinet decided it last week.' But as the Cabinet received poorer

N

advice so its decisions became more erratic and, often, impracticable. Impractical decisions, instead of being referred back for clarification, were quietly dropped. The Cabinet might forget all about them. As the expatriate civil servants disappear on a large scale, either by removal or because they are no longer able to do an effective job, and are replaced by inexperienced Africans, so the possibilities of effective action decline. This is not to say that there are no first-class African civil servants. There are, but they are swamped by the large numbers of the less able promoted, and they begin to find that they have no effective organization. They learn to live with inefficiency and with politics; with decisions which are erratic and unpredictable, let alone often impracticable. The capable African finds himself as handicapped as the capable European.

The influence of the immigrant races, one of our original factors in *uhuru*, is diminished to vanishing point. This diminution is aided by fear. Those who remain yield to pressures that would have evoked their indignation earlier. Nor is it clear where they stand or which group in the government will emerge as the dominant force. Fear was at play well before independence, as Asian house owners paid out money to Africans who declared that their houses had been earmarked for takeover, but that, if they paid so much, they would be allowed to keep them. Fear plays its part in the excessive Africanization in business, when companies are prepared to face a decline in efficiency in order to give a darker face to their staff, in the hope that they will be tolerated. Sometimes this is no more than a realistic approach to the new conditions. Fear has reduced the Kenya press to something less than purveyors of news. In the face of threats and warnings the press had decided to be non-controversial. But in a situation where the future is uncertain, where support for the government is the main hope of stability in potentially highly unstable conditions, all move with great circumspection, to put it at its best. One can never be sure that some politician will not secure one's deportation with no reason given. Club or bar stewards will be listening to European conversations and reporting them back. Europeans stop talking when Africans appear. One M.P. stated in Parliament that European farmers were deliberately running down their farms and evicting labour in order to make the government buy them out. He was forced to withdraw the remark as he could not substantiate it. In fact, all farmers knew that no action of that kind could get their farms bought. The M.P. later said that he had been told this by the bar stewards at a certain club where it had been said by some farmers. In this case, no doubt each party was correct in its statement and one can well understand farmers, late in the night, jokingly making some remark of this kind. Things like this have, however, made Europeans very wary of speaking when an African is present. Asians are more fearful, as they feel they are more vulnerable. They know that they can get no sympathy from India or Pakistan. Nor are they indispensable, since standards of efficiency have no priority. Their last fling was when, at the threat of more adverse conditions, over 1,000 Asian railway employees were persuaded to hand in their resignations in protest. This was an act which would have given the colonial authority pause. Their resignations were all accepted and they were sent back to India. Their leader, however, had not handed in his own resignation and remained. All this does not mean that conditions of living for Europeans and Asians are intolerable. In the need for circumspection they are no worse off than people in most countries, nor are they worse off than Africans themselves. It has, however, been interesting to observe Europeans warning those Africans who are inclined to speak their mind to be less outspoken and more careful of what they say. Colonial personal freedom has gone for all races.

It is, however, necessary that it should go. The country must be given purpose and direction. In a situation where the forces of disruption are so great, the government cannot tolerate a thousand voices of discord, which could make its problems more difficult to solve. It needs to create unity. The nation does not fall into line automatically behind the leaders when they become the government. The same disruptive forces work against and within the new government as against the old. New disruptive forces are added. In fact an African government is faced with immensely greater difficulties than a colonial government, even though many of them are of its own creating. But it creates them often unwittingly. The government begins to learn that it is not able to pursue even the most enlightened policies in a purely democratic situation, where a thousand cross-currents can change its direction. It has to work through others. As Cromwell had to dissolve Parliament in England's national interest after the revolution which had released all the forces at work within society, so the new leaders have to get a more effective control of everything if they are to pull the country through its difficulties. The one-party state is the modern equivalent of Cromwell's major-generals (although many countries, in a similar position, have followed Cromwell more closely). The one-party state has the virtue of preserving some appearance of democracy, although the organs of democracy are stifled, as the Caesars stifled the Roman senate, but left it in being.

One may question the way Britain has so assiduously exported to its colonies the mature Westminster forms of democracy. It has been suggested that the American version of these of two hundred years ago would be more suitable because they give stability to the executive. But it is doubtful if the American system is much better. Both are different versions of the same thing, and both depend on the respect for the law as the guardian of human rights and freedoms

and on conducting the political battle within the forms of
the law. Constitutions are not sacred in Africa. Britain herself has given Kenya a number of constitutions. They are no
more than political devices for shifting the balance of forces
within the country, not for establishing an immutable
structure within which those forces can play. The constitutions themselves have adjusted the balance of racial power,
and in so doing constitution-making has recognized the
basic problem within the country—the racial division. The
one-party state clusters round a single figurehead, an individual who symbolizes in his person the unity of the
nation, in much the same way as the Queen symbolizes the
unity of Britain. For those other Commonwealth countries
of which she is Queen she symbolizes a basic unity with
Britain, while for those who recognize her only as head of
the Commonwealth she symbolizes only a very tenuous
form of unity at all. In her own different statuses she symbolizes a double Commonwealth, with an inner ring and
outer ring. Symbols do symbolize. In America the constitution itself is the symbol of unity. African countries,
divided by tribe, with only a short history as a unit under
colonial rule, with no tradition of unity, have to build this
up. A leader of the opposition is not only a symbol of disunity, he can be a focus for the forces of disunity. It is
necessary to build unity around one person, who becomes
the personification of the nation. Criticism is an attack on
the nation itself and becomes a kind of treason. That is why
Mr Nyerere could not be dispensed with at the time of the
Tanganyika mutinies. To the people of Tanganyika far and
wide he was the Tanganyika nation. Without him, Tanganyika could have dissolved like the Congo. This is why,
too, Africans resent criticism of their chief leader. To insult
him, or to treat him in the same way as a Western politician,
is to insult them. Perhaps Britain, in exporting Westminster-
type constitutions, is as naïve as the Africans who expect

everything to go on as before, but with different persons in charge. It is difficult, however, to see what else could have been done. The demand for independence came in the name of democracy, of the right of peoples to choose their rulers by universal franchise. The fact that these methods must soon be replaced if the new states are to survive does not mean that they could have been set up with undemocratic forms.[1] This would have been as unpopular in Britain and America as in the East, which would have been unable to play its disruptive rôle fully, and would have denied the basic argument for independence. Africans, too, adhere to democratic beliefs until they find them against the national interest and, of course, against the interests of individual politicians, for an immense struggle for power takes place within a country after independence, a struggle that can itself destroy the country. This struggle for power itself is a struggle for control of the state and makes for unity of control. Even, then, if there were no national arguments for the one-party state there would be natural forces within the country tending to produce it. The respect for the law and the constitution is not so great that the struggle for power is not a struggle for complete power. African countries are in many ways fortunate when they go into independence with an accepted national leader, who has symbolized the achievement of independence and around whom national unity and power will be built. Such a leader, inheriting the goodwill and support of the people can be wiser than they. The extent to which he can be depends on how far he has to struggle to maintain his position and how quickly he grasps the need to control the physical forces in his country.[2]

[1] The popular vote gives the new government its legitimacy; it is a substitute for the hereditary factor in monarchy.

[2] Nkrumah's great service to Ghana was to give it unity. Presumably Mr Obote is trying to do the same in Uganda.

The problems of the leader

Let us assume that the leader is wiser and more experienced than his people, and that he identifies himself with the poorest of his people. This is perhaps an ideal leader, but it is very near the position in Kenya.

His problem is to control the disruptive forces in the community that have been released by independence, to harness them to a common purpose, to try to make the country take forward steps in development and above all to maintain his own position, since its hopes and aspirations centre on him and without him there is a serious danger of disintegration. He might expect, as some have done, that with all the homage he receives, his position is unassailable. It cannot, indeed, be assailed by popular vote, but his position as head of the country must be effective as well as nominal, and there are plenty of forces and individuals quite close to him who will be glad to wrest effective power from him while leaving him nominal authority.

He has to balance a number of conflicting forces, since if he is to do any good he must maintain peace. He must judge when to surrender a point to achieve some bigger end. He must try to encourage Europeans to stay and contribute what they can to the country, since he knows that if they go too quickly the economy will be destroyed. On the other hand he must show that he, too, is against them, or he risks unpopularity. He must work for inter-racial unity although no possibility of this exists. He must strengthen the armed forces, and he will know that expatriate officers will be more loyal and less liable to be corrupted than African, but they will be loyal to the law and not to him personally. They will not accept the expediencies that he is forced into. If, however, he maintains expatriates in the armed forces he will risk being called, outside his country, a European stooge and accused of employing white mercenaries. These cries will filter into his own army, already disappointed of posts that they had expected to gain, and lead to mutinies. Any encouragement to mutiny will fall on attentive ears. If he surrenders these posts then he must have a loyal security service answerable directly to himself which will keep him in touch with what is going on everywhere in the country so that he can forestall attacks and opposition. If he retains European security officers he will be accused of receiving biased reports and his actions in the government will be weakened because of this. If he has African security officers he will be in danger of their being suborned. He knows that if he lets the European civil servants get pushed out he will weaken his administrative machine and his chances of doing positive good for the country. With the tremendous natural pressure to get Europeans' jobs, allied to arguments about neo-colonialists, old colonialists and not being truly independent, he may be forced to let them go, if he is not to face even greater difficulties.

He will be aware that Communist influences are against him, without being told so by Mr Chou-en-Lai, and he will wish to control and restrict their activities. If he does, then, he lays himself open to charges of not being non-aligned. This important ideology can be influential, as it has seeped through all the lesser politicians to the people. If he were not to be clearly non-aligned then he would be subject to other attacks on a wide front. So the Communists must be given the run of the country, although he can use a false step, such as the army mutinies, to check them for a time. (It is important to remember that mutinying because one still has European officers and not their jobs, and because of Communist inspiration, are not mutually exclusive reasons, but in fact the one is the means by which the other is made effective. Little is known about what really was behind the mutinies, but it is significant that at Dodoma, in Tanganyika, mutineers rounded up Europeans at bayonet-point at night, held them and let them go, not knowing what to do with them. This suggests the issue of instructions, if not complete instructions, and its failure suggests the dual forces behind the mutinies. The troops were likely to rouse to mutiny on the European officer issue, but this did not in itself direct the mutiny in any purposeful way. A strike could have served that end.)

The leader must also acquiesce in visits by Communist aid missions, although they are likely to give him small assistance unless he is already virtually an agent of theirs, because his country is non-aligned and one of the accepted virtues of non-alignment is the possibility of playing off East *vs.* West. It seems likely that the West is more played upon than the East, since Communist aid is a small price to pay for gaining a foothold in a country, and (once there) technical assistance missions have an easy task playing on African anti-colonial feelings, leading them to think that everything from the West is bad, especially its best things, sowing doubts in their minds without actually advocating Communism itself, but rather that confused thing, African socialism. Why pay for European farms? Why not take them? (Who, then, can stop a reversion to subsistence agriculture?) Why go for individual holdings instead of following the traditional ways of the country through collectives? (This is a potent and highly disruptive argument. Traditional agriculture is individual not collective, although in a legal sense the tribe as a whole owned the land. Men lived on their holdings and not in villages. They were individualists. Each man wants his own piece of land. To put them in collectives runs directly against their natural impulses and is guaranteed to produce intense discontent in the future.)

The leader knows the strength of tribal feeling, particularly over land. He must be careful, certainly at first, not to arouse it and bring it down on his own head. He knows also that the overcrowded tribes cannot be bottled up in their own Regions indefinitely, or forces will be generated against him within his own group. There will be plenty to use these feelings to unseat him. How can he leave the Masai their empty agricultural lands when other tribes are starving? Yet he dare not provoke them until his own position is fully secured. In the meantime he has the European lands to offer. But they cannot be handed over too quickly.

He must have a South African boycott, even though this means more unemployment in an already desperate unemployment situation, and loss of trade and exports. He cannot get away with a nominal gesture, because too much feeling has been worked up on this. To the enthusiastic pan-African politicians what are a few thousand more unemployed? 'Men cannot live by bread alone.' 'We would rather starve than trade with South Africa' (said drinking pink gins before a sumptuous lunch).

There is a story told about the South African boycott which if not strictly true is exceptionally *ben trovato* and worth repeating. It seems clear that the Kenya Cabinet took the decision to impose a boycott on trade with South Africa after some hesitations in view of its likely effect on Kenya. It seems likely that the pressure from those who were East-inclined became overwhelming when coupled with the fear of losing face in pan-African circles, and that the convincing argument was that the East would make up in trade for that to be lost. Certainly Kenya immediately after the decision sent a strong trade delegation to the eastern European countries. It seems likely that they expected to be able to say: 'We have put a boycott on South African trade, but this is expensive for us, can you help us out?' expecting the east European countries to say in reply: 'Splendid, my dear chaps, now what can we do to get you out of your difficulties?' and not realizing that the East would be only too delighted to hear that the boycott was causing Kenya difficulties and so furthering their disruptive aims. The story is of the delegation in Poland. The Kenya delegates are reported to have made a statement similar to that above, and the Poles to have replied: 'What would you like to send us?' To this Kenya replied: 'Could you take some of our coffee?' (Eastern Europe counted as a 'new market' under the International Coffee Agreement and sales there were outside quotas.) The Poles said: 'Well, we might be able to; what would you like in exchange?' Kenya said: 'What would you like to send us?' To their surprise the Poles said: 'Dairy produce.' 'But,' exclaimed the Kenya delegates, 'we produce a lot of dairy produce ourselves; we export it all over the Indian Ocean area and even to Europe.' 'You mustn't believe that,' said the Poles, 'that is just imperialist propaganda.' 'No, indeed,' said Kenya, 'we have the Minister for Commerce and Industry here and he will tell you.' 'Yes,' said the Minister, 'you have only to look at the trade statistics.' 'Oh,' said the Poles, 'you mustn't take any notice of those figures, they are only lying British statistics.' An agreement for cultural exchanges was made. (Note 'exchange', not technical 'aid'.)

The leader must do all he can to reduce tension and keep hotheads under control. He must do something about the party youth wing or they could be a dangerous element, not only in themselves, but in other hands might become subversive of his own authority and a para-military group for seizing power or, at the least, for organizing demonstrations. They cannot just be disbanded. They must be found useful employment, and converted into a national youth service. He must be prepared to handle dramatic political gestures stirred up by elements that want to drive him in particular directions. The 'freedom fighters' is an example of this. It is also a significant story, because it misfired, and showed more divisive and self-balancing forces than its sponsors had expected. It is not clear who was behind the movement, which was supposed to be an attempt to bring these men out of the forests and turn them into national heroes. It was calculated to move the government leftwards and to arouse some alarm and despondency. The 'freedom fighters' seem to have been some tattered remnants of the Mau Mau who still resided high in the forests of Mount Kenya. The general public had been unaware of their existence and it seemed that they had simply become adapted to forest life and preferred it. They lived off the forest and by occasionally raiding the African farms below the forest. The political gesture was to call these men out as national heroes and give them land. The settlement authorities were told to find 800 plots for them on their schemes. They came out with ceremony. The local authorities receiving them, however, said that when they had weeded out all those who, on hearing the news, had gone into the forest and come out with them, in the hope of gaining land, and all those who already owned land but had preferred to live in the forests, it would not be necessary to provide plots for more than 50–100. Even so, finding plots proved difficult since the local Kikuyu selection committees objected strongly to their having any priority. 'We were detained,' they said, 'and since our release have worked with the government; why should these people who have stayed in the forest and contributed nothing to the country have preference?' Unfortunately for themselves and for the political gesture the 'freedom fighters' soon made themselves extremely unpopular by beating up the local people and expecting every privilege. Within a few months they were made liable to the law again and ceased to be heroes. Now most of them are back in the forest or in prison. The significance of the whole exercise is that it shows one of several attempts to shift the government to extreme courses by arousing popular feeling. In this case the popular reaction was badly misjudged.

Particularly, however, must the leader keep control of his

own government. His Cabinet-making is not unlike that of European prime ministers. He must satisfy powerful interests with a place in his Cabinet. This usually means those who have established a dominant position in a particular tribe. He must also take account of politicians who are supplied with foreign funds and who can buy support. So that in addition to the basic Cabinet of his own choice he must include members who may not feel great personal loyalty or may not understand the problems of government, as well as those who may be potentially hostile, while within the Cabinet will be many who are contending among themselves for power and influence as well as those who may seek to wrest power from him, without in fact disposing of him. He will have to decide when to give way and when he can stand firm, and will have to make concessions not in the country's interests.

This statement of the leader's problems is useful as indicating the conflicting forces at play after *uhuru*. It will be clear that it is an unstable situation in which clear and consistent policies cannot be applied; that a step forward may be followed by half-a-step back. In such conditions the fate of the man-in-the-street or the man-on-the-farm is liable to fluctuation if not lost to sight. Nor will these problems disappear with the one-party state although they may come more under control. Fundamentally the leaders of the governing party and the leaders of the opposition have more in common that they have with their followers.[1]

[1] This was written before the creation of the one-party state in Kenya.

CHAPTER EIGHT

The Balance Sheet

IT is now possible to begin to prepare a debit and credit account for independence, although it may be questionable if it has real value. To attempt to do so does, however, serve to bring out some of the underlying features.

On the credit side there must be a division between those who clearly gain from independence personally—our emergent African—and the masses. The one gets immediate gains; the other's gains, if any, lie in the future, and it is necessary to assess his prospects. And from what standpoint does one measure gain? Although man does not live by bread alone he cannot live without it. So we must consider economic gains as being significant to the people, and perhaps we can follow the Marxists in giving economic gains priority, especially as they are, to an almost equal extent, now given priority in the West. With increasing populations, the need to provide for them, let alone raise their standard of living, is important. Psychological gains must also be counted; status, a sense of society and stability and one's place in it, together with the opportunity that it offers.

Status

Status was derived in pre-colonial days from the conventions of tribal society, and its somewhat rigid structure was fully accepted, so that although there were strict limits to improving one's status one's position was established and changes in it took place, in a sense, automatically. Colonial rule had to some extent preserved this, through the system of indirect rule, and the provision of African 'Reserves' in which the traditional way of life was expected to go on. Colonial rule, however, also brought economic development in the towns and European farming areas, where traditional status concepts did not apply. This in turn spilt over into the Reserves, especially with land consolidation, and disrupted tribal society. In the towns a new status relationship was established based on race, with Africans in the third and lowest rank. As Africans went abroad more, with official encouragement, they went into societies where they were no longer in the third rank, and on their return felt frustrated. We have then three status positions; the traditional, which was breaking up in varying degrees in different parts of the country, particularly as money became a dominant factor which did not fit into the status arrangements of a subsistence society, but which still played a considerable part in the more 'backward' areas; the racial status positions of the towns and European farms which were, for a long time accepted by the majority; and the status positions of the 'emergent' African who could not accept the town position nor the traditional position, and hung in a sort of no-man's-land. All three positions were ones of growing emotional tension, which could lead in almost any direction but were, in fact, guided from outside (both East and West) into the independence outlet.

Independence has largely satisfied the status problems. It has fully satisfied those of the emergent African who is now dominant and can enjoy the discomfiture of Europeans and Asians. It does, however, fling him into a highly competitive world, for jobs, political position, etc. For as many as are satisfied there will be as many dissatisfied. This will serve to keep the struggle for jobs, position, influence going at full speed, and will lay the position open to foreign influence and funds, since there is no accepted principle, and the struggle is between men not policies. As an Asian commented: 'The African's trouble is that he has no religion or philosophy of life.' This results in the ready grasp of unphilosophical slogans imported from elsewhere—the African personality (it is no different from any other in its foundations), African socialism, pan-Africanism, non-alignment—all cries that appear to give purpose and, perhaps, dignity to African politics (and, indeed, are not much different from the slogans that people cluster behind in other countries). The danger of these slogans for the country is that they are not indigenous or related to its needs and that the new country is not sufficiently diversified, lacks the variety of interests of other countries, so that the slogans lead to harmful action and the personal power politics, instead of operating, as they do on a similar scale in Britain, within the bounds set by tradition and convention so that they are relatively harmless, in Kenya have themselves a highly disruptive effect. Kenya has lacked serious or original thought on its own problems, except by the colonial rulers. This is one more argument for the one-party state; to contain this ferment and to establish new channels of advancement and new conventions of status.

The status of the town masses has also improved; they may not be better off, but they feel equal to the other races and this gives them a sense of increased dignity and freedom. This sometimes emerges in hostility to other Africans giving themselves the trappings of the Europeans, the cars and chauffeurs, etc., and makes them responsive to attacks on African capitalists.

The traditional status positions in rural society are fading away as they are replaced by the new ones, although many ways and traditions will linger on. This will probably be quicker in Kenya than in countries where the tribes had a developed administrative machinery and where the tribe can provide an alternative status position. From the economic point of view the quicker the breakdown of traditional ways and the adoption of new ways the more hope there is for the country of economic advance, since the traditional ways were a severe brake on this.

Social stability and sense of society

Generally, then, as far as status is concerned, there is a large credit entry, although it is not a simple issue. With an improved status position has come an increased social instability. Mostly this was developing in any case under colonial rule and accelerating in the transition period. Only the instability of the political world is directly related to independence. A one-party state should do much to stabilize things in that sphere, and to enable the inherent instability of the countryside and the towns to be effectively controlled and suppressed, as it was under colonial rule. On the other hand this instability has been markedly increased by the economic effects of independence, in increasing unemployment and landlessness, and will continue to produce elements of danger for the government, elements that can be worked on to disrupt the country and that the government may not be able to find immediate measures to satisfy. It is significant that a large part of post-independence government thinking has been given to this; the tripartite agreement between employers and unions and the government, whereby employers undertook to take on an extra ten per cent labour in return for the unions undertaking to refrain from strikes; the move for youth works camps; and the more conventional search for foreign aid, not only to give development but also employment, and so replace the fall-off in capital investment (a big employer of labour) which had been caused by independence.

An early move must be to obtain control of the trade unions, one of the larger contributors to unemployment and discouragers of foreign investments. The unions have only one object; to increase the rewards of labour. This has been relatively easy in the past because the employers have

o

over-employed labour and not rationalized its use. It would be wrong to say that they have employed labour inefficiently since this depends (as we saw in considering output per acre *vs.* output per man in the agricultural field) on the criterion for measuring efficiency. At its old price labour was cheap and could be employed profitably in large numbers. It was, however, easy to increase wages in the face of union pressure and reduce the labour force. The unions provided, too, a political leader of a rather different kind, a rival in the towns for the tribal political leaders. In a state of desperate unemployment he was, however, working against the country's interests and increasing the instabilities with which the government must contend. For this reason it is necessary for the trade unions, too, to be absorbed into the one-party state. This will bring the union leader into the political free-for-all conducted within the party, but make him a part of the party hierarchy. He will seek his status within the party and not outside it. The unions will play the rôle they play in Communist societies and not that in capitalist societies.

On the question of social stability, then, independence greatly reduces it and increases instability. This can only be overcome by the one-party state, which introduces a new hierarchy and social structure to replace the old. It will also provide that sense of society and of 'belonging' which will give national unity. As independence approached we saw the sense of belonging being clearly established within the tribe, and the tribe establishing its position against other tribes. This will continue for a long time with the masses, although it is interesting to note that the tribal political leader has replaced the traditional authorities. This is due to the absence of a tribal administrative structure. For as long, however, as tribal ways are passed on to children at their mothers' knees, and tribal languages (the conveyors of culture) are spoken, the tribal loyalty will be a powerful factor.

For those further away from rural conditions, the loyalty and sense of belonging is transferred to the party. Where there is more than one party people will fail to find that sense of belonging. While, therefore, the leader must continue to balance powerful tribal forces, he must withdraw himself from tribal interests and attach a new loyalty and sense of society to himself and a universal party.

In this consideration of the sense of society we have seen, then, that independence does much to destroy it, and that it breaks up into tribal loyalties, which are strengthened, as the only repository, unless a national party is established to replace them, a greater rival for their loyalties with a ready-made group of followers in the already partly de-tribalized populations of the towns and European areas. The loss can be repaired. The tribal structure was breaking up, in any case, and colonial rule with a European settler community offered no alternative structure with any stability. A more positive policy by the colonial power of developing an integrated social structure (of which there was little evidence) depended on positive co-operation by the European community, which was absent, and, indeed, in spite of the many constructive minds, the European community pulled in the opposite direction.

Independence itself is more than a symbolic act, it establishes a change of social structure, a change with credits and debits, with a net credit at the end and a potential for a greater one. There was a degree of inevitability in it, although the timing depended more on outside influences quite unrelated to the stresses within Kenya's own society. Socially the new society offers something to everyone, although much more to some than to others. The concomitant of the one-party state is a lack of personal freedom and independence, a compulsion to conform, to think along certain lines and, perhaps, to be herded along certain lines. The disruptive forces are not destroyed; they are confined within the party. Although, therefore, there is a unity there is no certainty about the direction that it will take, or what ideology may eventually dominate the party machine. Will economic problems be dealt with in political terms? Will the people be driven into collectives instead of being allowed to have their own land? Will a one-party state develop increasing rigidities and lead to the emergence of a new, exploiting ruling class, with its evils mitigated by an enfeebled administrative machine? Will the search for easy answers to difficult economic problems cause them to be answered in ideological rather than practical terms, so that outside disruptive influences play their full part but within the party system? The one-party state, if it has no indigenous philosophy based on the country's own problems and facts, will simply hide the struggle without resolving it, and may continue to promote economic disruption.

The drawback to the one-party state is, of course, that it serves to conceal instabilities and may well not deal with them. It becomes a police state and, although initially its purpose is to repress some problems that are not immediately soluble, the tendency will be to suppress all problems. As instabilities and foreign interference increase, as conflicting counsels confuse, so will the one-party state tend to become a holding on to power, and not a solution to problems. Then only violent revolution can upset the state and offer the possibility of a shake-down into new equilibria.

The economy

What is the effect of independence on the economy? Here the tally is almost entirely debit.

The flow of capital ceases at the first mention of independence. With independence itself it begins to pick up again, but now it comes in a different form. Instead of flowing naturally into all the interstices and crannies of the community as opportunity offers, it comes in the form of formal foreign aid or large-scale operations.[1] Foreign lending is not of the kind that can concern itself with a mass of small

[1] Official foreign aid is becoming increasingly tied to the direct purchase of capital goods from the aiding country. This has recently become official British policy although, fortunately, in practice it seems less restrictive. If a country invests in development it will have to generate exports or import substitutes to cover: (a) the cost of capital goods imports over the period of loan repayment (hence the need for long-term loans and an eschewing of short-term export credits or contractor-finance unless the project is clearly going to generate exports or import substitutes to the right amount rapidly); (b) interest on the capital goods imports (hence the disadvantage of fixed-term borrowing against private equity investment); (c) the proportion of local costs that goes, in the first and successive rounds, on consumer goods (and other) imports; (d) the proportion of value-added (salaries, wages and profits) of the project in succeeding years that goes on consumer goods (and other) imports. All development investment creates a demand for imports considerably in excess of the actual import content of the project (this is recognized by the World Bank—probably alone among aid-giving agencies—and first round expenditure by the recipients of local cost expenditure is accepted by the Bank as qualifying for its loans). As many projects, particularly of the infrastructural or welfare kinds, do not generate exports or import substitutes to the extent required in the time required, it is not surprising that almost all developing countries have acute foreign exchange problems that lead to import restrictions, or that grants or 'soft' loans (longer term, lower interest rates and perhaps really non-repayable in effect) are becoming the centre of consideration. This effect of foreign aid is only balanced if the total import demand created by the aid, less the exports or import substitutes generated by the aid, is met by real saving within the aid-receiving economy. The more aid that is concentrated into a short time the more difficult it is to achieve this. Communist aid seems, in theory, to have an advantage on this point, if it is repaid in exports of primary goods, since it will not only widen the market for commodities in surplus in the producing countries but at the same time be likely, by so doing, to increase the return from capitalist markets in higher prices. It bristles, however, with administrative and political difficulties, including the gearing of part of the receiving country's economy to what can be a politically arbitrary, controlled economy. Perhaps the lesson for the West is not so much 'trade not aid' as aid related to trade.

investments, all demanding scrutiny and assessment. It looks for the large project and the large amount. The small entrepreneurs who risked their capital in various ventures have disappeared. Investment becomes related to the needs of the lender rather than of the country. This had always been a problem for Kenya, as the colonial government itself had pursued a policy of small, widely-scattered and diversified schemes and found difficulty in 'selling' these to foreign sources of aid. The Swynnerton Plan itself was really a bundle of small projects put together and synthesized. Development corporations offer a way of translating foreign aid into small schemes, but depend on the lender having confidence in the skill and expertise of the corporation's staff, and on the corporation having skilled and expert staff. This becomes more difficult to attract as time goes on since local conditions are uncertain. Foreign experts prefer to be recruited by outside agencies and lent to the country. In any case they lack experience of the country, and their advice is so much the poorer. It was always said in the Department of Agriculture that a new officer was of no real value for at least two years, and that is the usual term of secondment under technical aid schemes.

So, in addition to the fall-off in capital investment, and its change of direction, there is a lack of the skill to make use of it. It is true that one can expect more aid from more sources, but one still lacks the means to make it effective. This lack of means increases as time goes on, and crash training programmes of local staff do not automatically make good the lack. People can be trained to pass examinations and tests, but this does not make them effective in action. For this they need experience on the ground, working with those more experienced in translating knowledge into results. Those with whom they could do this disappear rapidly at independence, either with positive encouragement or because the environment in which they work has changed

so markedly that they feel unable to do a job. As the Europeans disappear from the civil service the burden on those
remaining increases until it becomes intolerable. The breakdown in administrative efficiency affects all work and nulli-
fies effort. In this situation the trained, experienced and
capable African is affected as much as the European. In
addition both will suffer political intervention which will
further reduce the will for results.

Although foreign aid may increase, then, the channels by
which it flows become clogged. The administrative machine
is like the channels of an irrigation scheme, as the capital is
like the water, bringing life and increased production to the
land. If the channels become clogged the water does not
reach the land, or does so fitfully and irregularly.

As independence becomes more real so a truly local currency system becomes necessary. A central bank is inevitable
and immediately the country is immersed in problems of
balancing its imports and exports, controlling its imports,
rationing its foreign exchange—delicate operations which
again require skilled experts. These are problems which
even advanced countries find difficult, and heavy-handed
operation of controls (even the existence of controls) introduces an arbitrariness into the economy which stifles enterprise. Who, when risking his capital, can foretell what
controls a government will impose, especially as these can
be used for ideological ends as well as economic ones?

With the weakening of the administrative machinery will
go a weakening of the highly geared development machinery of co-operatives and statutory organizations. As the
pressure on the European farmer grows (and we have seen
something of the forces that build up this pressure) so there
is the danger of the economy breaking down. Even the remaining European farmers, with an uncertain future, are
no longer developing the land.

The trends tending to weaken the economy far outweigh

those likely to strengthen it, and are likely to be accelerated as all the divisive and disruptive forces from outside are given full play. The possibility of the country attaining sustained economic growth seems remote and the probability is that the economy will gradually decline. It is a matter for speculation how far the decline in medical services and health services will offset this by keeping population growth within bounds. If it does not then there is a future for most people of increasing impoverishment, although, of course, many Africans will be richer. As statistics (and colonial statistics were notoriously poor) get poorer, some of the problems of government, the problems that face a conscientious and efficient administrative organization, will disappear. If you do not have information you do not know what problems you have to tackle or how to do it.[1] The feed-back of information, in statistical form, is the way that governments assess problems and decide how to deal with them. The problems do not disappear in reality; they become a different kind of problem. They require political guesswork and acumen, and are liable not to be tackled until they are already dangerous, because until then it is not known that they must be tackled. At that point the grand gesture, the big answer, is the only course open, and these are made in simple terms, creating new problems, setting the community off on new courses, without coming to grips with the original problem itself. As impoverishment increases, so the material available for both foreign subversion and for dissident or power-seeking individuals is increased and made more inflammable. Economic and social policy are removed from the plane of the interests of the people, and are considered on quite a different level. As

[1] Who now knows or, indeed, cares, whether the population of the Congo is increasing or decreasing, the people getting poorer or richer, as the Kasavubu–Mobutu–Tshombe triangle is formed and re-formed, and foreign interference ensures that no stable policy can be worked out?

we saw how British policy came to consider Africa in the context of its own international relations rather than in the interests of the people of Africa, so, within an African country, policies are decided on in a context quite extraneous to the interests of the people. The country is basically unstable. The main efforts of the leader must be to maintain stability; in doing so he must deal with the political forces that are stirring, taking decisions which give victory over this faction or appease that one. In this a coherent economic policy is lost.

The long-term prospect is one of a stable but weak state, with the potential for growth which existed under colonial rule turned into a decline; nature taking its toll of human life as it did in the past until a new equilibrium is reached at a lower level. This would be masked by foreign aid, foreign technical assistance, and slowed down by them. In 20–50 years Africa would cease to be of much significance to the rest of the world, except as a producer, on a reduced scale, of primary produce for the advanced countries. This picture, however, seems unlikely to be realized. As we saw, independence came at a greater speed than that generated by internal causes, because of outside influences and Britain's world policies; i.e. Britain's attempts to meet outside influences in its much weaker post-war condition. The same outside influences will not leave Africa alone. The new African governments are unlikely to be given the time to reach a new equilibrium. The unstable elements in the society will grow faster in the initial period, before the new balance begins to be reached. The one-party state, like foreign aid, is a check to the unstable influences, but they can still work within it, while foreign aid from too many sources will give outside influences a chance to cause disruption and confusion under official protection. It seems probable that the newly independent countries will fall under Communist control, particularly Chinese.

Communism an answer?

So far we have considered Communist influence as something hostile to our major concern, the interest of the people themselves. Is this necessarily so?

If we forget the general Western interest in keeping Communism at bay or confined, will Communism be harmful to Kenya? Drawing the conclusion that economically Kenya must go back and assuming, as we must, that colonial rule with its progress and development cannot return, is Communism not the only alternative which can now offer progress? Colonial rule, with all its limitations and slowness, was progressive and, given time, the internal forces would have compelled it to change its nature, but always just too late, so that greater tension would be created at each point than was satisfied. From the economic point of view it had far more possibilities than independence, and was more likely to ensure bread for the people. As far as their social needs were concerned it was backward, if not backward-looking. Independence reverses this; economically the country declines, socially it looks forward to the building up of a new social structure adapted to economic realities. No doubt at some point the two will meet and equilibrium will be restored if there is no intervention from outside. This cannot be, because Kenya needs the rest of the world and must, in effect, invite it to intervene. The rest of the world intervenes, not in Kenya's interest but because it has the opportunity of pursuing its own interests there. Kenya is bound to suffer from some form of 'neo-colonialism' from many sources. It is not simply that Africans are not clever enough to play off against each other the different intervening forces. The mere fact of inviting them puts them in a position to work on the internal disequilibria, themselves greatly increased by independence, before things have time to settle down into a new balance. To give itself time Kenya must side firmly with one or other of the two major outside influences, and exclude the other. To side with the West and exclude the East gives the possibility of ultimate stability at some lower economic level, but does so by denying the values of the West; personal freedom and democratic practices. This is because the East *versus* West struggle is already in Africa, and to take either side means suppressing the other. (The one-party state in itself is not an attempt to suppress either but to provide that national unity which can contain and replace both.) The West itself is confused and looks askance at allies that deny its principles, but less so than formerly, and its interest is more in allies in Africa than in democracy and personal freedom in Africa.[1] On the other hand it soon finds its allies are governments that increasingly depend on it for continuing in power. As they suppress more freedoms so they put the lid on more pressures and depend on outside support when the head of steam becomes dangerous. These governments are driven into their position willy-nilly and, as they lose both their economic and social *raison d'être*, become what they are labelled—vested interests supported by alien power. This is the dilemma of the West as it is of the African leaders. The one must, in supporting its interests, not only give ammunition to its enemy, but in fact support regimes that have become rotten (perhaps because of its support, since they cease, or are unable, to rely on themselves). The other, if it sides with the West must also give ammunition to the other side, and be charged with the stigma of 'colonialist stooges'. As the African leaders cannot solve their countries' problems in time, charges of this kind find plentiful support in widespread discontent, once the golden haze of independence

[1] This is the real 'sin' of the Smith regime in Rhodesia, not that it denies Africans freedom, etc., not even that it embarrasses Britain in its Commonwealth relations and at the U.N., but that it may strengthen the forces of the East, the disruptive forces, in independent Africa to the north.

wears off and hopes are disappointed. The disappointment of hopes leads to cries, not for new measures but more of the old ones—get the Europeans out quicker; give people land anyhow, nationalize this or that, and so on, all ultimately remedies inspired from the East that gathered concealed under the wing of independence. To maintain its position, the government will accede to many of these demands and further alienate its Western allies' sympathy, until, perhaps, the struggle is seen in the simplest terms as one of force, in which the African country concerned is an instrument of the cold war and no more, its inhabitants in the front line of others' battles.

Now suppose that the country aligns itself with the East instead. It is likely to receive more immediate, positive military and organizational help. It is possible that it will be able to renew its economic advance under the new organization which will be, and must be, much more ruthless than the gentle colonial regime, since it inherits a highly unstable situation. In this situation, of course, both independence and personal freedom vanish except in name and the name becomes a tattered thing. The Eastern rulers who replace the colonial rulers will be less experienced and more ideological, so that even economic advance, in agricultural countries, may be slower than hoped for, or even nonexistent, since the new rulers will have little real concern for it or the people. For these reasons, most African leaders are reluctant to throw in their lot with the East, especially as they would hold their own positions on sufferance and virtually surrender their leadership. In fact they do not do so, and the East makes its appeal to lesser leaders, anxious to take over power, who do not realize that in doing so they are surrendering it to their backers. It is this middle echelon of leaders that the East works on and who respond to it.

The middle course, of keeping outside both East and West camps, as we have seen, simply will not work. It produces all the worst possible results of siding with the West, but with greater sureness and speed. It is just possible that by siding with the West one can really keep the East out and maintain a modicum of freedom, some development and social stability, if one is determined to use force to maintain one's position, since force maintained over a long time can often effectively suppress subversion until the economic and social situations which give rise to it change. This, however, is only a slight hope.

Looking at the three possibilities, then, of siding with the East, siding with the West, or maintaining non-alignment, we see that the last is the most destructive position of all, both socially and economically. Non-alignment is the means whereby the East gets an extensive foothold in the country from which to work on and work up the disruptive forces within it until a slight revolution can topple the unstable edifice, and the East is in charge. No more is heard of non-alignment and oddly enough no one in the West today expects Zanzibar to be non-aligned. This is like the Roman Catholic approach to religious freedom; in democratic (and Protestant or agnostic) countries where it is in a minority, the Church claims liberty under the doctrine of the free state; in countries where it is in a majority it denies liberty to others under its own doctrines.[1]

[1] This statement was based on innumerable Roman Catholic pronouncements from Montalembert's statement: 'When I am weaker, I ask you for liberty because it is your principle: but when I am the stronger I take it away from you because it is not my principle'; to Ronald Knox in his *The Belief of Catholics* (1927): 'You cannot bind over the Catholic Church as the price of your adhesion to her doctrines, to waive all right of invoking the secular arm in defence of her own principles . . . is it certain that the Catholic Government of the nation would have no right to insist on Catholic education being universal (which is a form of coercion) and even to deport or imprison those who unsettle the minds of its subjects with new doctrines? It is "certain" that the Church would claim that right for the Catholic Government, even if

Of the two alternatives remaining, of siding with the East and siding with the West, the former offers a superficial economic attraction (if colonial rule must be abandoned then Communist rule offers the only hope to these ever-growing populations since they will be unable to develop themselves) but destroys personal freedom and status. The latter gives a chance of freedom and status, and may even cause as much economic progress as the former (who will ever be able to tell, if Communist statistics are anything like the Polish idea of British statistics?).

Independence may be unfortunate for the 'ordinary' African but, if his leaders are wise and have any regard for his interest, they will take shelter under the wings of the West. If they are more concerned with 'African personality' than the African they will have the worst of all worlds.

It would be unrealistic, however, to suppose that African countries can shelter under the wings of the West. Dr

---

considerations of prudence forbade its exercise in fact'; and on to Fr. F. Cavelli in *The Condition of the Protestants in Spain* (1948, quoted from the translation given in *Christianity and Crisis*, vol. VIII): 'The Catholic Church, being convinced by reason of her divine prerogative that she is the one true Church claims for herself alone the right to freedom . . . where material circumstances—whether the hostility of a Government or the strength of the dissenting factions—do not allow this principle to be applied in its entirety, the Church requires that she shall have all possible concessions. . . . In other countries, the Catholics are obliged themselves to ask for full liberty for all. . . . The Church does not in this way give up her theses, which remain the most imperative of all laws, but adapts herself . . .'

This strong, stern logic has great psychological appeal to many and is copied by the Marxists. It goes far to explain why Marxism is strongest in Catholic countries and why it is easier for the individual follower of one to convert to the other, rather than to less logical structures.

It remains to be seen whether the changes in this doctrine reported to have been decided at Vatican II do, in fact, herald any change in the real position of non-Catholics in Catholic-dominated countries or whether the Ethiopian's skin is still of the same colour underneath.

Banda may be able to try in Malawi and it might be possible for Zambia. In other countries it is too late.

At the outset we asked whether independence had come with the inevitability of a Greek tragedy. It should now be clear that the initial coming of the European and his impact on the area called Kenya did not lead inevitably to independence at this point of time nor to an independence of this kind. Perhaps Kenya has simply been shaken in the world kaleidoscope and taken a new position.

CHAPTER NINE

Postscript

I HAVE tried in the preceding pages not to unravel the threads that make up *uhuru*, so much as to describe them. To unravel—too clear an analysis—would belie the reality. By describing them one gives an element of confusion as a particular thread is described again and again in the different contexts in which it appears. At this point it has one effect; at another point a different one. It would be nice if I could now reduce it to a simple nutshell, explaining all in a few words; something that people could toss about with ease. This I cannot do. Africa may not be as dark as when the early explorers first visited it, but it is certainly more obscure. All things are complex and nothing is simple, but the obscurity of Africa is such that light shines on an occasional facet only and gives a false impression of the whole. I only hope that in this attempt to shine the light on as many facets as possible at once something of the real shape has emerged.

Any attempt to look at a complex scene such as this (and I pray the reader's indulgence for constantly changing the similes as I try to express different things) must have a point of reference; some point by which distances and directions are measured; some point by which events are assessed. My own should now be clear to the reader. In looking at the events that I have described my reference point has been what happens to the 'ordinary' African, in his millions, and in his hunger, in his attempt to live. I have not been concerned with the fate of Europeans in Africa except as they affect him. Nor have I been concerned with the African leaders except in the same way. I have taken no sides in the East *versus* West struggle, except as it affects the ordinary

African. I confess to being sad for him. Things that he knows nothing about, things that are irrelevant to his problems, will decide whether he eats or starves, whether he dies or lives.

A struggle is taking place which is not one between white and black but between East and West, although every effort is made to make it look like a black *versus* white struggle. Between these two millstones the 'ordinary' African is likely to be ground very small.

Africa presents especial problems for Christians who are asked to take sides in the name of their religion, of humanity, of charity. They see the distress and are often tempted by princes and leaders of various churches (have they a political golden calf hidden under their surplices?) to support this or that political creed. All the more credit then to those, missionaries, civil servants, farmers, etc., who continue in Africa to do constructive work and really deal with the 'ordinary' African; people who often literally give their lives to this end, as quietly and unobtrusively they get on with their job, a building job.

APPENDIX

Extract from a Speech of the President of the European Civil Servants' Association[1]

Those of you who were at our last General Meeting will remember the main reasons that we put forward for 'unity' which were that in a country bedevilled by racial controversy it was necessary to build up a solid core, in the civil service, of men of all races, united by a common loyalty and intent on serving the best interests of the country as a whole and giving it some stability. You will recall that we stressed the need to bind people of different races, as far as could be done, in new loyalties to each other, which would cut across and weaken the more natural alignments by race, which can only bring trouble as they have already done. I want to explain the development of our thought in this matter, so that it may be clearly understood why we have directed our attention so much to the principle of inducement pay.

In the past we had from time to time undertaken joint action, with the other associations, usually when we were so dissatisfied that we wished to make a demonstration. I am happy to say that since the inauguration of the Whitley Council such demonstrations have been unnecessary, and we have a lot to thank you for, Sir, for making this so. My precursor as President had negotiated with the other races, agreed proposals for a single clerical service of five grades, with Europeans entering at Grade I, Asians at Grade III and Africans at Grade V, except for special qualifications, with promotion right through for all, and further promotion on merit, with equal pay. There were sound reasons for this plan, although it is not logically perfect. Although we always regarded it as a large change which would need time and careful handling, it was simplicity itself compared with the Commission's proposals, and had the advantage of being already acceptable to the Service.

[1] 19 Nov. 1954, *The Civil Service Journal*, no. 144, Jan. 1955, pp. i. 23–30.

At first our Association had been a little doubtful about the proposals. We feared that they might result in no entry into the service for European boys, and we hesitated. The previous Governor, at our Annual General Meeting in 1950, told us that the proposal was premature. In 1951 the President of the African Association addressed our Council, and said (more or less): 'We regard ourselves as the leaders of moderate African opinion; we advocate working and co-operating with the Europeans; but if, when we advocate this, we always come back empty-handed, people simply laugh at us and go after the extreme agitators.' The thing that I want you to notice about this statement is the claim, which I think is well-founded, that African civil servants have a considerable effect on African opinion generally. A large part of the educated Africans is in the Service and they are nearer to Europeans than most of their fellows. They are something like Caleb and Joshua whom Moses sent out to spy out the land of Canaan, they report back what they find in the 'land' (or rather the character) of Europeans, and what sort of people we really are. It may be difficult now, with the Emergency between to remember what those days of 1950 and 1951 were like. There was increasing crime and lawlessness, there were African agitators, innumerable semi-rebellious sects, and to those who had any contact with Africans it was clear that they regarded themselves as oppressed and were thinking in terms of force.

We therefore applied ourselves carefully to the problem. We came to the conclusion that the solution was to try to remove the racial basis of our society and to try to establish a new country and nation of Kenya, which would attract the loyalties of all its peoples, who at that time regarded themselves first as Europeans, Asians or Africans. We felt that each race made a valuable and necessary contribution to the life and prosperity of the country and that the trend towards increasing racial hostility, which could only damage both its prosperity and its social life, could be resolved for the benefit of all. There was little that we could do, but we believe that the civil service sets the pattern of the country, so the Council unanimously agreed to set about the task in the one field that it could—the Service.

In June 1952 we published an article in the *Journal*, entitled

'What Sort of Kenya?', which embodied our views. Here are some extracts from it, and I would remind you that it was written more than six months before the Emergency when no one was expecting it and it was still being argued whether Mau Mau existed. We make no claim to clairvoyance, but drew some obvious conclusions from the way things were drifting:

The thing that most influenced members was the thought of what sort of Kenya was being built up and what it would look like in a few years' time when our children were taking their places in the world, if racial feeling were allowed to continue and to increase. This is undoubtedly a political matter, especially at this time, as well as a service matter. But we have no hesitation in discussing it as we form a large part of the white population in a country which we hope our children will regard as their own. If it were not a political matter it would be less urgent. The course that Kenya will take will be charted in the next few years. It is important that civil servants should consider this fully as a practical affair affecting their own futures. The race question is at the bottom of the future of Kenya.

We are already encountering an increase of crime, lawlessness and disaffection. The leaders of the African Civil Service regard themselves not only as civil service leaders but as leaders of Africans in general. They are the 'moderate' leaders who advocate working together with Europeans for their mutual advantage and not flying off to listen to the more extreme agitators that try to stir up, and thrive on, racial strife. They are men of good will who wish to turn Kenya into a country which is good for Africans (as well as Europeans) to live in, where the African of ability has an equal chance to make progress with the man of any other race. If, however, they advocate co-operation but always return empty-handed from trying it, they will soon loose their followers and these will turn to the extremists. This is only natural and probably most of us in the same position would feel the same. From this point the pattern of future events is easy to forecast. It can be seen in many other colonies. It is at this point that we come in, before the course is set, and must ask ourselves, 'What sort of Kenya do we want?'

If things go on in the direction in which they seem set at present, the Africans will turn more and more to the agitator, and we shall need more and more police to protect us from increasing crime, and then from increasing physical danger. At that point Kenya will have become a very uncomfortable place to live in. No doubt we have power on our side and could control the situation indefinitely, but that would not make it any pleasanter. More and more societies would be proscribed, more and more newspapers would be banned, and eventually a police state would be established in which every African would be regarded as a potential enemy (and hostility to Europeans a mark of patriotism for Africans) and fear would rule the lives of all races. Economic progress would probably be checked and investors, with the example of other countries before them, would have no confidence in Kenya. Such a country would be viable in its fashion. But such a course would be equally disastrous for all races. This is not a fanciful picture. The beginnings of it are around us already. Many of us, however, want to establish a British way of life here and such a country would be a travesty of it. It is in terms of force that the African already thinks and talks.

It is not necessary, however, for the gloomy picture, given earlier, to come true. It is not necessary for East Africa to give either a South African or West African answer to its problem. East Africa, because its circumstances are different, can have an East African solution. The alternative is to try to build a country in which the people are not Europeans, Asians and Africans in competition, but Kenyans working in harmony, a country where a man will be judged by his character and abilities as a man, irrespective of his race. Not all Africans are hewers of wood, and not all Europeans are leaders. Nevertheless the Europeans in Kenya tend to come from leader-stock. There should be no fear, if equal conditions were granted to Africans, but that the Europeans would still lead the country, but they would share their leadership with some Africans. The Africans should not expect preferential treatment, which they tend to ask for, nor should they be held back when they show ability. It will perhaps be the Asian who will have more difficulty in losing his Asian-ness. In such a society the good African would have as great interest in controlling the bad African as anyone else. In such a country it would be possible for Europeans (like any other Kenyan) to live happily without fearing others, and we could then return to the time, not so long ago, when it was not necessary to lock and bar one's house in Africa, nor keep a revolver, nor need women and children fear to go out alone.

That, as far as I know, is the first published statement on what is now called the 'multi-racial society' but which we called the 'non-racial society'.

By this time the Whitley Council had been set up and the Staff Side, composed of four of each race, had settled down amicably to deal with its common problems. From time to time we tell the others not to be damned fools and from time to time they tell us. There is no spurious pious goodwill here—it is hard business wherein we consider that the greatest benefit to each race depends on working together. The Africans and ourselves have occasionally had to help, and sometimes shove rather violently, the Asians over some of the non-racial fences. But when they have picked themselves up on the other side they have usually seemed quite glad to be there. Their main fear seems to be of being squeezed out between the other two, and then they wonder whether they shouldn't fight as a minority, which, of course, is the surest way of being squeezed out. We next set about preparing the ground, first by the Public Service Commission, to ensure that our proposals would be fairly applied and so that they would be seen to be so. We were just ready to table our proposals for a non-racial service when the Salaries Commission 'broke' on us. We had at that time no reason to suppose that they would do more than revise salaries, certainly not turn the Service topsy-turvy, especially as our own negotiated proposals were at that time known to Government.

This year the Lyttelton constitution was set up, which, in general, was so near our own ideas, that we expected no further problem, and you can imagine our dismay when we saw the Salaries Report. It is necessary to be quite clear about why we differ from the Commission over inducement pay. Our main arguments you will have seen in our Memorandum. As I understand it, from the Governor's speech at the opening of Legislative Council, the Government argument is this: 'We are establishing a non-racial service by having the same basic salary for all races, but owing to the extra expenses of officers from overseas and our need for them we must induce them to come here with something extra.' This is a fair enough argument *in vacuo* but when you try to see how it will work it doesn't fit the realities of the situation. In the first place a great number of recruits to non-inducement pay posts have come, not from the locally-born or domiciled, but from the exodus from the Army, the O.E.T.A.s, and the Groundnuts Scheme, and it is very unlikely that they would have come on local terms being offered now. Nor do we think that the true local European will come into the Service and work beside someone from overseas in the same job at much lower pay. This, we admit, is conjecture, but it receives confirmation from an interesting source. The Africans and Asians both were of the opinion that the local European would disappear from the Service. It was a strong temptation to them to accept inducement pay, in order to get rid of the local European, and eventually all Europeans. It would also give them a perpetual grievance, and a perpetual grievance is not a thing to be thrown away lightly, as it became clear that the result of the arrangement was Europeans (admittedly expatriates) on one rate of pay, Asians and Africans on another. However they both resisted temptation and stood by the ideas that we had worked at together, realizing that a service of disappearing Europeans at the top and Asians and Africans underneath would not be a non-racial service, nor would it be in the interests of the country, which depends on all races for its development. I hope, too, that we can take it as a tribute to the sincerity and honesty with which our Association has always dealt with the other Associations. It is often not realized that Africans and Asians deeply distrust Europeans (and each other), and I am afraid not without some cause. They hear fair words and expect fair action, but often find that there was an unexpressed reservation behind the words. In fact they are crying out for honest and straightforward leadership. I think one of our claims on their trust lies in our non-racial proposals not being a direct result of the Emergency but antedating it by a long time.

We think therefore, that there will be no place for local Europeans in the service of their country in the future, except by various devices whereby they can get into a limited number of jobs carrying inducement pay, that inducement pay which is necessary for overseas officers because of their extra expenses. You will be interested to know that Africans and Asians will also be able to get it in those jobs. The net effect is that inducement pay is unconnected with the extra expenses of overseas officers, is unconnected with market values; if you are appointed by one board you get it, if you are appointed by another board you don't. We are happy to say that the Asians and Africans have fully supported us in this, in spite of what you may have read some time ago in the *Standard* about their accepting the Report, and we are glad to think that in this country, where there is so much talk of multi-racialism, we have, in one sector at least, been able to breathe some reality into the idea.

Index